SPY SITES OF NEW YORK CITY

by

H. KEITH MELTON AND ROBERT WALLACE

with

HENRY R. SCHLESINGER

TO OUR READERS

New York City is a city of mystery, adventure, spies, and intrigue. As you retrace the steps of American patriots and traitors, we hope you will catch the sense of danger and exhilaration that are part of the secret world of espionage.

Through every era of American history, New York City emerges as a hub of espionage—where secrets are created, stolen, and passed through clandestine meetings and covert communications. Some spies do their work and live long, successful lives, while others are compromised, imprisoned, and—a few—executed. None has a certain future.

As you explore the nearly 200 New York sites where spies lived, plotted, and operated, recall that they walk the same streets as you, exchange greetings as they pass by, and never betray their true mission. They are as ordinary as any stranger you will encounter today.

We hope the brief stories presented here will whet your appetite for history and encourage you to identify more great spy sites in New York or in the community where you live. If so, take a picture of the site, write a fifty-word description of why it is significant, and send it to us at *coolspysites@gmail.com*. If we include your site in a future edition of this guide (or that of another city), we will acknowledge your contribution and send you an autographed copy of our latest Spy Sites work. In case of duplicate submissions, just as with spies, the first accurate report receives the glory.

Above all else, remember all is not as it seems—enjoy the adventure!

H. Keith Melton
Robert Wallace
www.spy-sites.com

CONTENTS

KEY

DOTS ARE COLOR CODED BY ERA AND INDICATE MAP LOCATION:

- Revolutionary War (red)
- Civil War (black)
- World War I (green)
- Between World Wars (yellow)
- World War II (orange)
- Cold War (blue)
- 21st-Century Spying (purple)

MAP ABBREVIATIONS:

UM - UPPER MANHATTAN	QU - QUEENS
MT - MIDTOWN	BX - THE BRONX
LM - LOWER MANHATTAN	BR - BROOKLYN

PREFACE

A SAYING GOES "NEW YORK WILL BE A NICE TOWN ONCE THEY GET DONE BUILDING IT."

There is seemingly no end to construction and reconstruction in New York. In a city that relishes and rejoices in the new and the novel, buildings are built, torn down, and rebuilt with unfailing regularity. The famed grid system that divided the city into regular blocks without concern for topography–first developed in 1811 to ease the way for development between 14th Street and Washington Heights–did not include a large section of Lower Manhattan. Consequently, 18th-century addresses invariably are a tricky matter. They may not correspond exactly to present day addresses, but they do offer a general approximation of the location.

The resulting ambiguity about exact coordinates of some of the espionage operations described in *Spy Sites of New York City* is consistent with the uncertainty integral to the spy's profession. How do you know if a coffee shop conversation is actually a plot to overthrow a government or if a clothing store is the cover for a spy ring? Can you be certain the chalk mark on a mailbox is graffiti? Or is it a signal that a dead drop has been loaded? And are the two middle-aged moviegoers genuinely interested in the feature film, or are they looking for a dark location to exchange briefcases loaded with secrets?

While experiencing more than two centuries of New York spy sites, keep in mind that while the buildings, streets, businesses, alleys, and hotels may have changed, the excitement, intrigue, and danger of espionage still surrounds you—in fact, the stranger standing next to you right now might be a spy on a mission.

In compiling this guide, we are indebted to the support of a host of friends and colleagues in America's intelligence and counterintelligence services who prefer to remain unnamed. Our literary agent, Daniel Mandel, and our counsel, Brian Wainger, were consistent in their encouragement and sound guidance as the project developed. Mary Margaret Wallace and Melissa Schlesinger reviewed the manuscript to make it more reader friendly and grammatically correct. Intelligence historian Hayden Peake offered invaluable knowledge of New York and 20th-century espionage. Peter Earnest, executive director of the International Spy Museum, and Oleg Kalugin, retired KGB major general, who both served as intelligence officers in New York, generously provided introductions and shared in our enthusiasm for producing this work.

To you, the reader and traveler in these adventures, we are deeply appreciative of your interest and trust that our guide will enliven your experience of New York City.

THE EXCITEMENT, INTRIGUE, AND DANGER OF ESPIONAGE STILL SURROUNDS YOU—THE STRANGER STANDING NEXT TO YOU RIGHT NOW MIGHT BE A SPY ON A MISSION.

A KGB SPY EYES NEW YORK

"If I can make it there,
I'll make it anywhere,
It's up to you, New York, New York . . . "

That's how Frank Sinatra put it in his highly romantic and unforgettable song. For the intelligence services of all nations, New York has always been the center of attraction. Viewed as the heart and mind of America, it symbolizes the power of the great country and its immense potential.

I came to New York in 1958 as a member of the first group of Soviet students in the U.S.A. after World War II. The group's chief was a war veteran and senior official of the Soviet Communist Party. The rest, including myself, were young intelligence officers or KGB informers.

When I came back to New York on my second assignment, undercover as a Radio Moscow correspondent at the United Nations, I learned that the total number of KGB intelligence officers exceeded one hundred in New York alone. The Soviet UN mission, trade, and consular officials, journalists, and of course, the United Nations secretariat served as good camouflage for spy activities. There were no known illegals, although the KGB residentura had a deputy resident in charge of illegal operations. In 1962, when Rudolf Abel, convicted in the U.S.A. for espionage, was exchanged for U.S. U-2 pilot Gary Powers and glamorized in the USSR as a hero, it became obvious that the illegals were still in demand.

In fact, the end of the Cold War and the collapse of the Soviet system had little effect on the spy activities against the U.S.A.

True, there were setbacks and defections, but Russian espionage never ceased. The U.S.A. became "target #1" instead of "enemy #1," and illegals were dispersed around the country, their primary mission being to obtain information and technology helpful to the Russian "modernization program." For decades, Russia benefited from its natural resources and fell behind in know-how, compared to Europe, China, and the United States. The brain drain—emigration of high-class specialists—also contributed to the deterioration of the Russian cconomy. It's no wonder that economic and technological espionage had to be revitalized.

A major spy scandal in 2010 involving Russian illegals—and their subsequent exchange for several persons jailed in Russia for espionage—is the best illustration of what has been going on behind the slogans about "resetting Russian-American relations."

New York is renowned for its geographic diversity and is therefore highly conducive to spy efforts. Manhattan was always the preferred location—primarily for personal meetings with targeted individuals and active human sources. Intelligence officers avoided downtown, Harlem, and Chinatown (too many tourists and cops), but Riverside Drive and the adjacent park zone north of 75th Street were viewed as convenient for dead drops and brief personal contacts. One of the preferred meeting places was Upper Manhattan, a mile or so south of the Bronx. Another favorite was Yorkville, with its German descendants and good beer.

Occasionally, spy operations were conducted in Brooklyn, Queens, and New Jersey, but these locations were not recommended because getting there inevitably involved using bridges or tunnels controlled by the police. Still, the prevalence of Russian-born or Russian-speaking people residing in some parts of Brooklyn were operationally inviting.

In my time, Soviet intelligence used technological devices sparingly to maintain contact with their human sources. To look into the eyes and read a person's soul was the preferred modus operandi.

New York, in that sense, provides unparalleled opportunities for comparisons, mental and spiritual exercises, and emotional outbursts—from fury and disgust to delight and admiration. And that's what professional spies (or recruiters in a general sense) are looking for to eventually achieve their goals. As the song says, "If you can make it there, you'll make it anywhere . . ."

—OLEG D. KALUGIN, KGB MAJOR GENERAL (RETIRED)

A CIA OFFICER EYES NEW YORK

Manhattan. April 6, 1978. Late.

Heart pounding, sweat pouring down his arms, the middle-aged Soviet official jammed clothes into his overnight bag, took a last look at his sleeping wife, slipped an envelope containing a note and some money under the bedroom door, eased the apartment door closed, and fled. Frantic, he tore down twenty flights of stairs, stumbling and stopping to catch his breath at every other landing before finally reaching the ground-floor exit to 64th Street.

Gasping for air, he spotted the sedan waiting down the street—his salvation, unless the driver flashed the lights to warn of danger and the need to abort the operation. Steeling himself, he looked quickly up and down the streets. Even now, might a waiting KGB killer step out from the darkness and end his flight with a well-aimed bullet or the slash of a knife?

UN Under-secretary-General Arkady Shevchenko was a protégé of Foreign Minister Andrei Gromyko and a rising star in the Soviet Ministry of Foreign Affairs. However, deep in his Ukrainian soul, Shevchenko had grown to hate his ministry bosses, the ubiquitous KGB minders, indeed, the whole Soviet system. Two years earlier, he had secretly volunteered to be a clandestine source for the CIA. The telegram from the Ministry recalling him to Moscow a few days earlier meant that he had fallen under suspicion. The game was over. Tonight he would become the highest-ranking Soviet diplomat ever to defect to the United States during the Cold War.

Shevchenko's alienation from the Soviet Union, his secret approach to the Americans, and his dramatic defection–all took place in New York City. His life in the city had profoundly affected him and his ultimate decision to seek freedom.

Now the Cold War is over and the era of globalization is upon us, but our fascination with spies and their "tradecraft" has never been stronger. Whether in books, movies, or TV, we follow intently the intriguing tales of the more than 500 spies recruited by the Soviets in America before World War II, or more recently, the ten Russian illegals rounded up in 2010.

New York City, one of the world's great international cities and host to the United Nations and hundreds of other organizations representing foreign countries, is a magnet for the world's intelligence services–all hunting potential agents and sources and using the well-honed tools of their tradecraft to manage or "run" them.

As you explore New York's five boroughs, imagine you are an intelligence officer from another country, sent here to recruit sources of intelligence–individuals who will agree to enter into a clandestine relationship with you and provide secret or "classified" information, sometimes at risk to their lives.

As an intelligence officer, you are constantly looking for out-of-the-way places to meet and develop close relationships with potential sources and prospective recruits. As you walk New York's streets, ride its subways, and sit in its parks, you are always making notes of meeting places that don't appear suspicious, like restaurants and coffee shops, but where you believe your meetings will not be observed by local law enforcement or your potential source's colleagues.

The real challenge emerges once you have recruited the source and must devise ways to stay in contact with him without accidentally alerting counterintelligence officers—either American or your source's. This is where your judgment and tradecraft are vital. Can you maintain contact by secretly meeting in a safe house or even a car at night? Or would those places be too risky? Does your source's security require "impersonal means" of communication so that the two of you never appear in the same place at the same time?

Impersonal communication may require "dead drop" sites, places where the source can hide his material in a concealment, such as a hollow brick, in an area where it will be undisturbed. If so, he will need an innocuous way to signal you that he has "filled" his dead drop, just as you will need to signal him that you have "unloaded" it. The signals between you and your source could be as simple as chalk marks on a telephone pole, a book carefully positioned in the rear window of a car, or a flowerpot on a balcony.

A riskier tradecraft technique is the "brush pass," a technique in which you and your source arrange to pass by each other quickly ("brush") at a crowded subway stop at a time when you have calculated the encounter is not likely to be seen by observers who might possibly be hostile. The life of a spy is always dangerous, and events can turn deadly in an instant.

For the first time, two intelligence historians have dug into the elusive files and records of espionage to identify the secret sites integral to major spy cases in New York City since America's beginning. Their work, *Spy Sites of New York City*, lets you match wits with master spies as you retrace their footsteps on the streets of New York—hunting sources and running them. Spies have been doing this throughout our nation's history. And as we know, they still are . . .

—PETER EARNEST, RETIRED CIA OFFICER AND EXECUTIVE DIRECTOR, INTERNATIONAL SPY MUSEUM

REVOLUTIONARY **WAR**

During the Revolutionary War, New York City saw relatively few battles, yet was the center of major and dangerous spy operations by both Patriots and British. General Washington learned the consequences of discovery and capture early in the war when his spy Nathan Hale was caught by the British. Hale's execution served as both cautionary tale and inspiration for those early Patriots. Even if a suspected spy managed to escape the hangman, the notorious British prison ships anchored in the harbor and the makeshift prisons of converted warehouses and sugar refineries often amounted to a different kind of death sentence–that of disease and slow starvation.

Despite enormous risks, George Washington, America's first spymaster, understood that winning the war depended on secret intelligence. His "confidential correspondents," operating clandestinely inside British-occupied New York City, employed the tools of classic tradecraft, including dead drops, signal sites, commercial covers, invisible ink, ciphers, numbered code names, and aliases. So good were their covers and tradecraft that the identities of some of Washington's most valued agents remained a secret well into the 20th century.

PATRIOTIC SPY AND HERO

CAPTAIN NATHAN HALE STATUE

City Hall Park at Broadway, Park Row, and Chambers Street

Tall, easily recognized by powder burns on his face, and unconvincing in his disguise as a Dutch (New York) schoolteacher, Nathan Hale was untrained, ill-equipped, and, by many accounts, unsuited for espionage. According to one witness, a wily British officer easily tricked Hale into confessing his mission. Still, the young Patriot achieved American hero status after the British hanged him without benefit of a trial or clergy rites on September 22, 1776. More than two centuries later, the specifics of his secret mission have long been forgotten by most Americans, yet the failed Revolutionary War spy is known to every schoolchild for his last words, "I only regret that I have but one life to give for my country." Unfortunately, history has also obscured the precise location of his execution site.

A plaque adorns the ***Yale Club, 50 Vanderbilt Avenue at 44th Street,*** (1) proclaiming it to be the site of the execution. After all, he was a Yale graduate, class of 1773. The location is less than precise–in 1948, the Yale Club plaque was transplanted from its original location of *46th Street and First Avenue* when the slaughterhouse on which it was mounted was torn down to make way for the United Nations. Most likely, Captain Hale was hanged near ***66th Street and Third Avenue*** (2) at what was then the Park of Artillery, adjacent to a popular watering hole called the Dove Tavern. A nearby plaque commemorates Hale on the building's ***Southwest corner of 65th Street and Third Avenue.*** (3) Regardless of the actual location of Hale's death, a statue depicting a stoic Hale facing execution stands at ***City Hall Park at Broadway, Park Row, and Chambers Street.*** (4)

"I ONLY REGRET THAT I HAVE BUT ONE LIFE TO GIVE FOR MY COUNTRY."

–Attributed to Captain Nathan Hale

WHAT DID HALE REALLY SAY?

Whether Hale actually spoke those famous words on the gallows is a matter of debate. A British officer who witnessed Hale's hanging wrote that Hale said, "It is the duty of every good officer to obey any orders given him by his commander in chief."

A newspaper article published six years after Hale's death reports the words as "I am so satisfied with the cause in which I have engaged, that my only regret is that I have not more lives than one to offer in its service."

The legendary quote "I only regret that I have but one life to lose for my country" is taken from the memoirs of Hale's friend William Hull.

Brooklyn-native Frederick William MacMonnies won the competition to sculpt the thirteen-foot-tall Nathan Hale statue while still in his twenties. The statue was unveiled in 1893 on what was then thought to be Hale's execution site.

AMERICA'S FIRST "STAY-BEHIND" AGENT

HAYM SALOMON

Sugar House Prison, 34 and 36 Liberty Street (then called Crown Street)

Following General Washington's retreat from New York in 1776, Jewish immigrant Haym Salomon, or Soloman, remained, working for Washington's fledgling intelligence service as a "stay-behind" agent. A member of the Sons of Liberty, Salomon sheltered American spies and escaped prisoners in his New York house. When the British swept into New York, Salomon was apprehended and confined to a sugar refinery, called the ***Sugar House, 34 and 36 Liberty Street.*** 5 Salomon's ability to speak multiple languages impressed the British commander, and he was handed over to General von Heister, commander of the Hessian mercenaries. Von Heister thought he was getting an interpreter. Instead, Salomon, who was still loyal to Washington, continued spying. Arrested again in 1778 and sentenced to death, Salomon bribed one of the guards and escaped to Philadelphia, where he became a major financier of the war.

The Sugar House Revolutionary War prison was a converted warehouse where inmates were crowded together, provided meager rations, and denied medical attention. It's been estimated that those taken prisoner by the British forces during the Revolutionary War suffered a 50% mortality rate.

REVOLUTIONARY WAR SPECIAL OPS

KNOWLTON'S RANGERS

Columbia University's Mathematics Hall at 2990 Broadway, between 117th and 118th Streets

This plaque commemorates an early victory for Washington's troops against the British on September 16, 1776.

Lt. Colonel Thomas Knowlton, a native of Connecticut and veteran of the French and Indian War, was selected by George Washington in August of 1776 to form Knowlton's Rangers, an elite company for conducting reconnaissance missions behind enemy lines. A month later, on September 16, 1776, the British discovered Knowlton's scouting party. Badly outnumbered, the Rangers at first retreated through what is now Upper Manhattan. However, they regrouped to fight valiantly after becoming enraged when a British bugler rallied his troops by mockingly sounding the foxhunting call *Gone Away,* traditionally used to signal a fox in full flight. Washington ordered reinforcements, who eventually succeeded in pushing back the British troops. Known as the Battle of Harlem Heights, this first victory in the war under Washington's command proved costly–Lt. Colonel Knowlton was killed.

According to the Connecticut Society of the Sons of the American Revolution, Knowlton was buried with full military honors in an unmarked grave at what is now ***143rd Street and St. Nicholas Avenue.*** 6 Plaques commemorate the battle throughout the area, including one on ***Columbia University's Mathematics Hall at 2990 Broadway, between 117th and 118th Streets,*** 7 and another in the small park across from *Riverside Church at Riverside Drive and Claremont Avenue between 120th and 122nd Streets.*

TURTLE ATTACK

AMERICA'S FIRST MILITARY SUBMARINE

West side of the Battery in Lower Manhattan

Designed and built by Connecticut inventor David Bushnell, the *American Turtle* was the new nation's first fully submersible submarine used in combat. Constructed from oak, the spherically shaped, one-man vessel featured a small conning tower on top. Powered by a hand crank and screw propeller, the only navigation was by way of a small porthole and compass.

On the night of September 6, 1776, Sergeant Ezra Lee boarded the *Turtle* on the ***west side of the Battery in Lower Manhattan.*** 8 His mission: to sink the British warship HMS *Eagle* and break the British blockade of New York. Bushnell had discovered that dynamite could be detonated underwater, so he designed an explosive device that would screw into the hull of the ship from the submerged *Turtle.* When he reached the *Eagle*, Lee descended beneath the water line and made multiple unsuccessful attempts to attach the bomb. Despite the operational failure, New York City can rightly claim honor as the launching site for history's first wartime submarine attack.

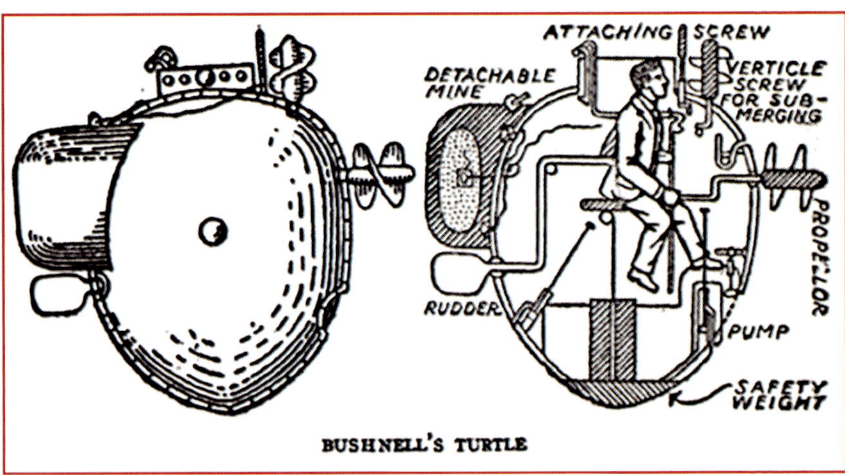

The American Turtle submarine, invented by American Patriot David Bushnell, proved ineffective when launched against a British ship in New York Harbor. The hand-crank-powered craft illustrated unconventional warfare tactics by those fighting for independence.

LOOSE LIPS AT THE TAILOR SHOP

MULLIGAN BROTHERS

23 Queen Street (now Pine Street)

Although married to the niece of a British Royal Admiral, Hercules Mulligan was a staunch Patriot and member of the Sons of Liberty. With his brother Hugh, the Mulligans were agents of the Culper spy ring, running an espionage operation under the business cover of a fine clothier at *23 Queen Street (now Pine Street).* 9 The shop featured "superfine cloths of the most fashionable colours" and more significantly "epaulets for gentlemen of the army and militia." British officers who frequented the Queen Street shop were measured and fitted for their uniforms by Hercules himself. As the officers selected material and stood for fittings, they gossiped about troop strengths and movements. In one instance, Mulligan observed British officers ordering particularly heavy clothing, indicating a movement north to the colder climate of Quebec. This vital information was quickly passed to the revolutionaries.

At the end of the war, Washington rewarded Mulligan's loyalty not with a bag of gold–the usual payment for spies–but by buying a full set of clothing from the shop. Thereafter, the business thrived, boasting signs and advertisements reading: "Clothier to Genl Washington." Hercules and Hugh are buried in the *Churchyard at 74 Trinity Place at Wall Street.* 10

Hercules and Hugh Mulligan played active roles in the American Revolution as members of the Sons of Liberty and operatives of the Culper spy ring. They are buried in a crypt in the Trinity Church cemetery, not far from their friend Alexander Hamilton.

PRINTER TO THE KING AND MOST EXCELLENT SPY

JAMES RIVINGTON

Northeast corner of Wall Street and Pine Street

A bookseller turned newspaper publisher, James Rivington published an unabashedly loyalist newspaper on the ***northeast corner of Wall Street and Pine Street.*** 11 The *Royal Gazette* billed its owner as "Printer to the King's Most Excellent Majesty" and seemed to go out of its way to taunt New York City Patriots in an effort to undermine the Revolution. Under the motto of "Open and Uninfluenced," Rivington published rumors, outrageous lies, and even challenges to the Sons of Liberty. The *Royal Gazette* proclaimed George Washington fathered illegitimate children and was secretly plotting to turn the new nation Catholic. Other stories falsely reported Benjamin Franklin was on his deathbed and France's King Louis XVI was destined to be crowned King of America if the Revolution succeeded. Widely mocked and even burned in effigy, Rivington kept on printing the inflammatory stories. Finally, in May of 1775, a mob of enraged Patriots gathered outside his printing plant. They smashed the press and carried off the lead type to melt down for bullets.

[NEW-YORK, WEDNESDAY, February 12, 1783.] [No. 666.]

THE ROYAL GAZETTE.

PUBLISHED BY JAMES RIVINGTON, PRINTER TO THE KING'S MOST EXCELLENT MAJESTY.

SUGAR HOUSE PAPER, TO BE SOLD. Enquire of the PRINTER.

SWORDS, CUTTEAUX, AND PISTOLS, Of various Kinds.—To be had of the PRINTER.

THE MOST BEAUTIFUL CANES, In great Variety for GENTLEMEN and LADIES.

POLLOCK and URQUHART, Have commenced the Business of INSURANCE BROKERS. IN which Line, all Orders will be punctually attended to at their Office, No. 16, Great Dock-Street. January 1, 1783.

TO BE LET.

WAX CANDLES.

ASBY and HUTCHINS,

LENTE'S STORE, HAS FOR SALE.

NEW-YORK, FEBRUARY 12.

His MAJESTY's most gracious SPEECH to both Houses of Parliament, on Thursday, December 5, 1782.

Received on Sunday last, by the Brigantine Peggy, Captain M'Neil, in 19 days from Tortola.

Which was brought to Tortola, from Windward, by Captain Rodney, Son of Lord Rodney.

My Lords and Gentlemen,

SINCE the close of the last sessions, I have employed my whole time in the care and attention which the important and critical conjuncture of public affairs required of me.

I lost no time in giving the necessary orders to prohibit the further prosecution of offensive war upon the Continent of North America. Adopting, as my inclination will always lead me to do, with decision and effect, whatever I collect to be the sense of my Parliament and my people; I have pointed all my views and measures, as well in Europe as in North America, to an entire and cordial reconcili-

the gallant defence of the Governor and garrison of Gibraltar; and my fleet, after having effected the object of their destination, offering battle to the combined force of France and Spain on their own coasts; those of my kingdoms have remained at the same time perfectly secure, and your domestic tranquility uninterrupted. This respectable state, under the blessing of God, I attribute to the entire confidence which subsists between me and my people, and to the readiness which has been shewn by my subjects in my city of London, and in other parts of my kingdoms, to stand forth in the general defence. Some proofs have lately been given of public spirit in private men, which would do honour to any age, and any country.

Having manifested to the whole world, by the most lasting examples, the signal spirit and bravery of my people, I conceived it a moment not unbecoming my dignity, and thought it a regard due to the lives and fortunes of such brave and gallant subjects to shew myself ready on my part to embrace fair and honourable terms of accommodation with all the Powers at war.

I have the satisfaction to acquaint you, that negociations to this effect are considerably advanced, the result of

Reviled publisher James Rivington was actually a spy for the Patriot cause. While his paper printed slanderous stories about George Washington, Ben Franklin, and other Patriots, Rivington clandestinely provided a steady stream of intelligence to General Washington from British-occupied New York.

Alexander Hamilton tried, unsuccessfully, to stop the mob. George Washington called for restraint. But in short order, Rivington was back at the presses, his newspaper again publishing incendiary messages. With the British occupying New York, he also opened a coffee shop that sold portraits of the king, stationery, and writing accessories. The store became a favorite among British troops because, despite wartime privation, Rivington somehow managed to keep it stocked with delicacies.

The secret source of supplies was Rivington's very silent partner, Robert Townsend of the Culper spy ring, and his Patriot business contacts who kept the coffeehouse well stocked to lure in the British soldiers. From his military patrons, Rivington compiled intelligence tidbits, which he jotted down in invisible ink on blank pages bound into books or inserted into sheets of writing paper purchased at the store and delivered directly to General Washington. So perfect was his cover that for more than a century following the Revolution Rivington was reviled almost as much as Benedict Arnold. Rivington's role in the Patriot cause remained hidden until historians in the 1950s uncovered his efforts in the Revolution through forensic analysis of his handwriting and paper samples.

Robert Townsend's role in the Culper spy ring wasn't uncovered until the 1930s. Only one known image of the secret Patriot exists, drawn by his young nephew, Peter, in the early 1800s. Today the portrait resides at the Raynham Hall Museum in Oyster Bay, Long Island.

After retirement, Rivington lived at ***114 Pearl Street***, 12 He died on July 4, 1802, and was buried at the ***Middle Dutch Church at Nassau Street and Cedar Street.*** 13 The church no longer stands–the spy's remaining monument is ***Rivington Street***, 14 which runs between *Bowery and Pitt Street on the Lower East Side.*

THE SONS OF LIBERTY DRANK HERE

FRAUNCES TAVERN

54 Pearl Street

This meeting place for the Sons of Liberty and site of George Washington's farewell address to his officers is still called the Fraunces Tavern and is one of New York City's historic treasures. It boasts a restaurant, bar, and museum.

Samuel Fraunces purchased the Queen's Head inn and tavern at *54 Pearl Street* 15 in 1762. He changed its name at the start of the Revolutionary War. The tavern became a regular meeting place for the Sons of Liberty and later served as General George Washington's last residence in New York City. In the tavern's Long Room, Washington delivered his farewell address to his officers on December 4, 1783. A short time later, when New York was the Nation's Capital, the tavern housed the Departments of Foreign Affairs, War, and Treasury.

Was Samuel Fraunces (called Black Sam) a spy? Maybe. What's known for certain is Fraunces came from the West Indies and remained loyal to Washington throughout the Revolution. The strongest hint of his role as a spy can be found in the grant voted to him by the New York State Legislature and Congress for aiding American prisoners of war and undefined "other services."

One story of those "services" involves Fraunces's daughter, Phoebe, who worked for a time as George Washington's housekeeper. Phoebe is said to have uncovered a plot by one of Washington's bodyguards, Thomas Hickey, to assassinate the general in 1776 with a plate of poisoned peas. In another version of the story, Fraunces, not his daughter, discovered the plot. Regardless of the source, Hickey was executed.

Damaged by fire in 1844, the Fraunces Tavern was purchased by the Sons of the Revolution and reopened in 1907. The historic landmark became the target of a deadly terrorist attack by the radical Puerto Rican independence group FALN in 1975. Today, the Fraunces Tavern and four adjacent buildings house a museum of 18th-century New York exhibits.

THE PATRIOT'S MASTER SPY

CULPER RING HEADQUARTERS

Peck Slip, east side of street near Pearl Street

This busy waterfront street was a natural location for a store that secretly supported the Patriots.

After Nathan Hale's execution, George Washington knew he needed better spies and tradecraft. He turned to General Charles Scott and Major Benjamin Tallmadge for help. Tallmadge, a classmate and drinking partner of Hale's from Yale, was hit particularly hard by the execution. Along with Scott and Abraham Cooper Woodhull, a farmer from Setauket, Long Island, he formed the Culper Ring. Culper, according to historians, may have been a shortening of Culpepper County, Virginia, where Washington once worked as a surveyor.

Each member of the ring received aliases as well as code numbers for secrecy and communications. Washington's number was 711, Tallmadge, 721. Communications were based on a code Tallmadge devised. In a series of relays, information flowed from New York City through Queens, then across the Long Island Sound by whaleboat to Connecticut, and on to Washington's headquarters in Morristown, New Jersey. Nearly everyone in the ring was related by blood, marriage, or lifelong friendship. Key to the operation was Robert Townsend, number 723, alias Samuel Culper Jr., a New York City merchant. His store was a favorite among British officers who could afford its good assortment of lemons, rum, and quality dry goods. Although not a patron, General Washington was also fond of the enterprise, since it secretly served as a clearinghouse for intelligence dispatched out of New York City.

Townsend's store at *Peck Slip on the east side of the street near Pearl Street*, 16 also served as his home, and from it he penned pro-British writings for James Rivington's *Royal Gazette*. General Washington well understood the value of the store's cover.

"Sir, It is not my opinion that Culper Jr. (Townsend) should be advised to give up his present employment," America's first spymaster wrote:

> *I would imagine that with a little industry he will be able to carry on his intelligence with greater security to himself and greater advantages to us, under cover of his usual business, than if he were to dedicate himself wholly to the giving of information.*

Using an invisible ink called *sympathetic stain* or *white ink*, concocted by James Jay, the physician brother of John Jay, Townsend sent a steady stream of secret intelligence from New York to General Washington. As spymaster, Washington showed an intense interest in the smallest elements of tradecraft, providing detailed instructions on how Townsend should write his secret reports.

> *He should occasionally write his information on the blank leaves of a pamphlet, the first, second, and other pages of a common pocket book, or on the blank leaves at each end of registers, almanacs, or any new publication or book of small value. He should be determined in the choice of these books principally by the goodness of the paper, as the ink is not easily legible unless it is on paper of good quality.*

Townsend, a secretive man and lifelong bachelor, never spoke or wrote of his role as a spy. His identity as Culper Jr. remained a mystery until the 20th century.

WHO WAS AGENT 355?

A mystery agent–a female member of the Culper Ring–is mentioned just once in documents from the time. Known only as 355, her identity has been the subject of debate and speculation. Was 355 the mistress of the brooding Robert Townsend? According to legend, Townsend's lover was arrested and put aboard the prison ship HMS *Jersey*, where she gave birth to Townsend's child. Even as she was dying of privations, the mysterious mistress managed to keep the Culper Ring's secrets. Another account holds that agent 355 was a member of the coterie of women who trailed after the charming Major André as part of New York City's Tory high society. Less romantic, but more likely, is the theory that the elusive 355 was Anna Strong, a neighbor of one of the Long Island members of the Culper Ring. Recruited to enhance the cover of her partner, the pair would pose as an everyday married couple, allowing them to enter and exit New York City without suspicion.

UM17

CODES, CIPHERS, AND CANNON THEFT

ALEXANDER HAMILTON RESIDENCE

Convent Avenue and 143rd Street

The 18th-century building that Alexander Hamilton owned was named after his grandfather's estate in Scotland. Moved in 1889 and in 2008, the house has been meticulously restored by the National Parks Service and is open to the public.

As General Washington's aide-de-camp, Alexander Hamilton, who would eventually become the first treasury secretary of the United States, was responsible for decrypting letters from the Culper Ring. Equally intriguing is Hamilton's relationship to the Patriot brothers Hercules and Hugh Mulligan. Hamilton boarded at the Mulligan home on Water Street (between Burling's Slip and the Fly Market Slip, now part of the South Street Seaport) when he first arrived from Nevis, West Indies, and attended King's College (now Columbia University). In 1775, Hamilton, the Mulligan brothers, and other Patriot volunteers participated in a daring midnight raid to seize British cannons from the Battery in Lower Manhattan. The rebels came under fire from the HMS *Asia,* which was moored in the harbor. Once the Revolution heated up, Hamilton joined Washington's personal staff. In Hamilton, the Mulligan brothers and their spy ring had a trusted friend and confidant close to Washington.

A simple monument marks Hamilton's tomb on the south side of Trinity Church. Born out of wedlock and orphaned at age 11, Hamilton became aide-de-camp to General Washington and was intimately involved in espionage operations. On July 12, 1804, Hamilton was killed in a duel with Aaron Burr.

The only home Hamilton ever owned sat on his 32-acre estate at ***Convent Avenue and 143rd Street.*** 17 His family sold the house in 1889. In 2008, the 298-ton structure was moved a few hundred feet to its present location at the north end of *St. Nicholas Park*. After undergoing extensive renovation by the National Parks Service, it opened to visitors in 2011. Hamilton, a Founding Father, a contributor to the *Federalist Papers*, a secretary of the treasury, a diplomat, and a congressman, is buried at ***Trinity Church at Trinity Place and Wall Street.*** 18

THE POET SPY

MAJOR JOHN ANDRÉ'S HEADQUARTERS

1 Broadway, the Kennedy Mansion

The Kennedy Mansion was headquarters for both British and Continental Army officers, depending on who held Manhattan.

Major André, adjutant-general of the British Army under General Sir Henry Clinton in New York, was described as handsome, witty, charming, poetic and "possessed of a shining spirit." He selected John or James Anderson for his alias and ran spy rings from **1 *Broadway, the Kennedy Mansion*** 19 and the ***Beekman Mansion, called Mount Pleasant (demolished in the 1870s) at 351 East 51st Street.*** 20

André ran a number of successful agents, including Ann Bates, a schoolteacher from Philadelphia who was the wife of a British field artillery repairman. Bates knew armaments and military terminology better than most soldiers. Using the alias Mrs. Barnes, she infiltrated American troop encampments disguised as a peddler. For two years, between 1778 and 1780, outfitted with goods and suitably dressed, Bates enjoyed unrestricted movement among the soldiers as she carefully rationed her inventory to acquire as much information as possible to report to André at British headquarters. Her success is apparent in one of her reports: "I had the Opportunity of going through their whole Army Remarking at the same time the strength & situation of each Brigade, & the number of cannon with their situation and weight of Ball each cannon was charged with." Bates's intelligence, in part, prompted British General Henry Clinton to send reinforcements to Rhode Island, forcing American and French armies to withdraw following the Battle of Quaker Hill in 1778.

André's operations ended following a meeting with his most important agent, Major General Benedict Arnold, commander of the American fortifications at West Point. After a lengthy negotiation, Arnold agreed to surrender West Point, where a great chain restricted British ship movements up and down the Hudson River. In exchange for the traitorous act, Arnold would receive a British commission as a brigadier general, a lifetime pension, and several thousand pounds. After their final meeting, André was apprehended out of uniform with incriminating documents from Arnold hidden in his boots.

Washington convened a board of seven senior officers to try André on charges of being a spy. On September 28, 1780, the board found André guilty and sentenced him to death by hanging, a sentence partially motivated in retaliation for Nathan Hale's execution four years earlier. The decision was controversial because André claimed, truthfully, that he had been left behind enemy lines when his transport sloop, the *Vulture*, came under fire and left without him. Abandoned in hostile territory, André asserted he was not spying, but rather attempting to escape back to British lines, and was thus justified in wearing civilian clothing. Washington even proposed a swap of Major André for Benedict Arnold, but General Howe, commander of the British forces, refused the offer, sealing the young British officer's fate.

André appealed to Washington for a soldier's execution by firing squad, but the appeal was rejected. The 29-year-old André was hanged as a spy on October 2, 1780, in Tappan, N.Y. Alexander Hamilton wrote of him: "Never perhaps did any man suffer death with more justice, or deserve it less."

"NEVER PERHAPS DID ANY MAN SUFFER DEATH WITH MORE JUSTICE, OR DESERVE IT LESS."

– Alexander Hamilton

According to eyewitness accounts, André calmly tied his handkerchief for a blindfold with these last words, "Only this, gentlemen, that you all bear witness that I meet my fate like a brave man." Buried in Tappan near the gallows until 1821, his remains were reinterred in the middle of a little-used aisle in London's Westminster Abbey.

WHO CAN BE TRUSTED?

BENEDICT ARNOLD

Residence, 5 Broadway

Following his traitorous acts at West Point, which resulted in the execution of Major André, Benedict Arnold fled first to Philadelphia and then moved into a New York residence at *5 Broadway.* 21 Now a brigadier general in the British army, he began raising his own troops from among the Continental Army's deserters. He offered signing bonuses and tailored uniforms to those joining what he called the "American Legion."

In the fall of 1780, Arnold became the target of one of General Washington's most daring espionage operations. Conceived by Major Henry "Light-Horse Harry" Lee, father of Civil War General Robert E. Lee, the operation envisioned kidnapping the despised Arnold and bringing him to justice. The plan: a Virginian, Sergeant Major John Champe, was to fake desertion, join the American Legion, and capture the unsuspecting Arnold as he went on his customary evening walk.

The operation began well. Champe moved freely around New York in his new British uniform and established clandestine contacts with other Patriot agents eager to see Arnold hanged. However, the plot collapsed when Arnold's troops unexpectedly sailed for Virginia on the night of the scheduled kidnapping. Champe was forced to desert a second time, making his way back to General Washington's headquarters.

A year later, Washington sent another agent into New York City undercover as a deserter. This second spy, Sergeant Daniel Bissell, successfully joined Arnold's American Legion in 1781. For over a year, spending some of that time in an unheated hospital after falling sick, Bissell gathered intelligence on British troop strength, fortifications, and operations. He was the last recipient of Washington's Badge of Military Merit, receiving one of only three awarded by Washington himself.

Arnold survived the war, but he never escaped the shadow of the dashing Major André, to whom he was constantly compared, and whose death for the Tory cause was viewed as honorable and heroic. A harsh critic of Arnold at the time called him a "mean mercenary, who, having adopted a cause [Colonial] for the sake of plunder, quits it when convicted of that charge." Despised in the new United States, Benedict Arnold settled in England, which he disliked, and died in London in 1801. He was buried without the military honors normally befitting a British brigadier general. Still reviled by the country he betrayed, the invocation of Arnold's name remains a treasonous insult more than two centuries later.

AMERICA'S FIRST SPYCATCHER

JOHN JAY'S BIRTHPLACE

66 Pearl Street

John Jay

Jay was born December 12, 1745, at a no longer identifiable specific address of *66 Pearl Street* 22 on the site of one of New York's earliest landfills. Called "Water Lots," the area's construction expanded the buildable area in Lower Manhattan before redevelopment replaced the original structures. He would later reside at *133 Broadway (then between Cedar and Liberty Streets).* Jay played critical roles in the American Revolution, was a major contributor to the *Federalist Papers,* and became the first Chief Justice of the Supreme Court. Jay, like Alexander Hamilton, recognized the value of intelligence and in *Federalist Papers #64* promoted the necessity of spies by the executive branch of government.

> **"DISTRUST NATURALLY CREATES DISTRUST, AND BY NOTHING IS GOOD WILL AND KIND CONDUCT MORE SPEEDILY CHANGED."**
>
> **– John Jay, *The Federalist Papers***

The noted jurist got his start in counterintelligence as chairman of the New York State Committee and Commission for Detecting and Defeating Conspiracies. In this position, Jay oversaw scores of investigations–including one that uncovered a conspiracy to assassinate General Washington–as well as plots to sabotage New York's infrastructure. Through his brother, James, a physician and chemist in London, American Patriots got their first shipments of invisible ink, then called sympathetic stain or white ink.

Jay also ran his own spy networks during the Revolution. One of those involved Enoch Crosby, who operated in the so-called neutral ground that extended from Upper Manhattan north into Westchester County. This small stretch of land was "neutral" only in the sense that it was not held consistently by one side or the other.

It was from Jay's accounts of Crosby's exploits that James Fenimore Cooper gathered ideas for America's first espionage novel, *The Spy,* and its protagonist, Harvey Birch. Crosby later recounted his own espionage adventures in the memorably titled book, *Spy Unmasked; Or, Memoirs Of Enoch Crosby, Alias Harvey Birch, The Hero Of Mr. Cooper's Tale Of The Neutral Ground: Being An Authentic Account Of The Secret Services Which He Rendered His Country During The Revolutionary War. (Taken From His Own Lips, In Short-Hand.) Comprising Many Interesting Facts And Anecdotes) Never Before Published.*

CIVIL **WAR**

Although New York was more than 100 miles from the bloody battlefields of the Civil War, the city felt its effects. Its prominence as a financial and news center in supporting the Union cause attracted spies from the North and South who ran aggressive intelligence operations throughout the hostilities. Counterfeiters, privateers, and celebrities were among the city's Civil War intelligence operatives. In one major plot, a handful of Rebel conspirators set fires in hotels up and down Manhattan in an ill-fated effort to throw the city into chaos and possibly change the course of the war.

SPIES "HEARD IT THROUGH THE GRAPEVINE"

OLD GRAPEVINE TAVERN

11th Street and Sixth Avenue

Built in the 18th century, The Old Grapevine Tavern was housed in a three-story clapboard house at *11th Street and Sixth Avenue.* ❶ Originally called the Hawthorne, the tavern later acquired its better-known nickname from an ancient grapevine growing on one side. Popular with actors, writers, artists, politicians, and New York's fashionable men, The Old Grapevine became a Civil War gathering spot for Union officers as well as Confederate spies. The common phrase "heard it through the grapevine" is said by some to have originated at the drinking establishment.

Destroyed in 1915, The Old Grapevine, a hotbed of espionage during the Civil War, was described by the *New York Times* as "a favorite among actors, bankers and fashionable men about town."

The tavern was sold in 1912 and, much to the previous owner's dismay, opened a back parlor where women could sit and drink. The Old Grapevine was demolished three years later, in 1915.

UNDERCOVER CONFEDERATE SLAVE

MARY ELIZABETH BOWSER

Old West Farms Soldiers' Cemetery, Vyse Avenue and (approx.) 982 East 180th Street

You'll find a tree and a memorial plaque to honor freed slave and Civil War spy Mary Elizabeth Bowser in the *Old West Farms Soldiers' Cemetery, 180th Street* ❷ in the Bronx. Bowser worked with Elizabeth Van Lew of the abolitionist Van Lew family of Richmond, Virginia, providing intelligence on Confederate plans. In this tandem operation, Van Lew assumed an eccentric persona that earned her the nickname "Crazy Bet" among Richmond society unaware of her role as a spy. Bowser assumed the identity of Ellen Bond, a slow-witted slave generously loaned out to Varina Davis, wife of Confederate President Jefferson Davis. Bowser eventually worked as a servant in the White House of the Confederacy. When her cover was blown in January of 1865, Bowser attempted to set fire to the Confederate White House before fleeing. She then escaped, vanishing from sight. After Bowser's grave was discovered in Richmond in 2000, she was inducted into the Military Intelligence Corps Hall of Fame in Fort Huachuca, Arizona.

The Old West Farms Soldiers' Cemetery in the Bronx includes a memorial tree to commemorate the service of Mary Elizabeth Bowser during the Civil War.

HANGED AS A SPY AND PRIVATEER

JOHN YATES BEALL

Castle Williams on Governors Island

Joining the Confederate cause as a young man, Beall received wounds that rendered him unable to serve in combat. To continue his anti-Union fight, he became a privateer—a private person who attacks ships during wartime. Working the waterways along the Great Lakes, he made his way into the Chesapeake Bay, near Washington. Captured by the Union army, Beall was exchanged in a prisoner swap. He wasted no time returning to privateering and plotting to free Confederate prisoners. When he was recaptured, Beall was confined to ***Fort Lafayette*** ❸ on a small island just off Brooklyn's Bay Ridge section. Beall was tried as a spy and privateer in 1865. Six U.S. senators and ninety-one members of Congress interceded unsuccessfully on his behalf. He was executed on a hillside near ***Castle Williams on Governors Island*** ❹ on February 24, 1865.

Confederate spy John Yates Beall on the day of his execution on Governors Island. The gallows were within sight of Lower Manhattan.

Castle Williams, a three-tiered fort constructed in 1811 on Governors Island, was known as the "Cheese Box" because of its nearly circular shape. It became a prison for captured Confederate soldiers during the Civil War.

A UNION SPYMASTER

GENERAL GEORGE H. SHARPE

31 East 39th Street

A lawyer, diplomat, and soldier, George Sharpe began the war as a captain, was soon promoted to colonel, and in 1863 was made head of the Union Army's Bureau of Military Information. Under his direction, the U.S. Army began the modern practice of intelligence analysis, which included organizing and comparing information from a variety of sources before passing it up the chain of command. Sharpe's system included interviewing prisoners of war and refugees, retrieving papers from fallen Confederate soldiers, and monitoring supply lines with a network of "guides." One of Sharpe's most valuable sources was the Elizabeth Van Lew network in Richmond, Virginia, which successfully penetrated the Confederate White House.

By the war's end, Sharpe was a brigadier general stationed with General Grant's headquarters at City Point, Virginia. At Appomattox, he oversaw the granting of parole certificates to the soldiers of the Army of Virginia after General Robert E. Lee's surrender.

Union spymaster General George H. Sharpe created innovative new techniques for acquisition and analysis of wartime intelligence.

Following the war, Sharpe was appointed special agent to the U.S. State Department and sent to Europe to investigate Americans connected to Lincoln's assassination. He returned to New York and his law practice while holding a number of government jobs, including surveyor of the port and U.S. marshal for the Southern District of New York State. In the latter position, he investigated the corrupt Tweed Ring and Tammany Hall run by William Magear Tweed. Sharpe died in January of 1900 at ***31 East 39th Street.*** 5

LM6

"A VAST AND FIENDISH PLOT"

SETTING NEW YORK ABLAZE

P. T. Barnum's American Museum at Broadway and Spring Street

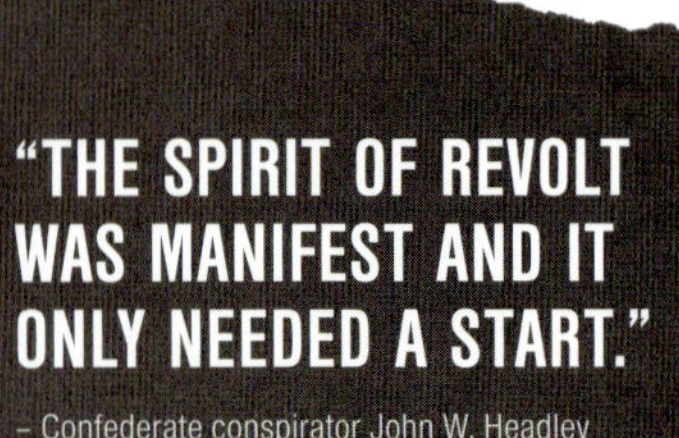

As General Sherman marched on Atlanta in the fall of 1864, eight Southern agents plotted to set fires in strategic hotels across New York in the hope of triggering chaos, seizing federal buildings, and freeing Confederate prisoners to overrun the city. One of the conspirators, John W. Headley, wrote, "The spirit of revolt was manifest and it only needed a start."

Fortunately, a Union double agent carrying messages between Richmond and Canada alerted officials, and President Lincoln ordered 10,000 troops into the city under the command of the notorious General Benjamin "Beast" Butler. Despite the obstacles, the conspirators met in a cottage in the unfinished Central Park and vowed to proceed with their plan. With twelve dozen bottles of Greek fire, a self-igniting fluid that spontaneously combusts when exposed to air, they began setting fires.

On November 25, 1864, small blazes erupted around the city including at the *St. James Hotel (Broadway and 25th Street), the Fifth Avenue Hotel (Fifth Avenue and 24th Street), the Lafarge House (Fulton and Pearl Streets), and the Howard Hotel (Broadway and Maiden Lane).* In all, rooms in nineteen hotels were set on fire as well as ***P. T. Barnum's American Museum at Broadway and Spring Street*** **6** and some hay barges in the East River. The chemical compound ignited as planned, but the inexperienced arsonists left the hotels' windows closed, starving the Greek fire of the oxygen it needed to spread. As a result, hotel employees and the fire department extinguished the fires quickly.

> **"A VAST AND FIENDISH PLOT TO BURN DOWN OUR EMPIRE CITY GAVE RISE TO THE MOST PROFOUND EXCITEMENT AMONG ALL CLASSES OF OUR CITIZENS."**
>
> *–The New York Herald*

The *New York Herald* reported the ill-conceived effort thusly: "A vast and fiendish plot to burn down our Empire City gave rise to the most profound excitement among all classes of our citizens."

All the conspirators escaped, except for the unlucky Robert Cobb Kennedy, who was apprehended in Detroit, tried, sentenced to death, and hanged at ***Fort Lafayette*** ❸. Reportedly, before the trapdoor opened beneath him, Kennedy sang, "Trust to luck/trust to luck/stare Fate in the face/for your heart will be easy/if it's in the right place . . ."

DEATH SITE OF THE BESTSELLING SPY

ALBERT RICHARDSON

Astor House Hotel, west side of Broadway between Vesey and Barclay Streets

As a reporter for Horace Greeley's abolitionist *New York Tribune* newspaper, located at what is now *One Pace Place*, Albert D. Richardson went behind Confederate lines during the Civil War, ostensibly to cover the war. Secretly, he was acting as a spy for the Union. Captured and imprisoned, he escaped and returned to New York to write two bestselling books: *The Secret Service, the Field, the Dungeon, and the Escape* and *A Personal History of Ulysses S. Grant*.

Albert Richardson

Richardson's daring success in the face of the enemy may have served to embolden his scandalous private life, and in November of 1869, he was shot by Daniel McFarland, the jealous husband of actress Abby Sage McFarland, in the *New York Tribune*'s offices. The mortally wounded Richardson was carried to the ***Astor House Hotel on the west side of Broadway between Vesey and Barclay Streets.*** 7 As Richardson lingered near death, Mrs. McFarland—who had obtained a hasty divorce—and the journalist spy were married in a dramatic deathbed ceremony. The murder trial of Daniel McFarland created a 19th-century media frenzy until the politically well-connected defendant was acquitted.

CONFEDERATE CURRENCY COUNTERFEITER

WINTHROP HILTON

11 Spruce Street

With the Civil War in progress, New York printer Winthrop Hilton found a profitable sideline in printing high-quality "novelty" replicas of Confederate currency. When millions of dollars of Hilton's bogus Confederate bills, printed at ***11 Spruce Street,*** 8 began flowing south, the genuine Confederate currency was devalued.

Two Confederate agents were dispatched to New York where they forged a letter—written in easily broken code—and saw that it came to the attention of the authorities. The letter cleverly alleged that Hilton was employed by the Confederacy to print genuine currency. In 1864, authorities raided the print shop and found millions of dollars in Confederate funny money. Imprisoned, but eventually released, Hilton ceased printing bogus Confederate currency.

A SPY ON THE STAGE

LM7

PAULINE CUSHMAN

Astor House Hotel, Broadway between Vesey and Barclay Streets

After the Civil War, actress and spy Pauline Cushman donned a Union soldier's uniform to recount her exploits before packed houses in New York.

For a brief period in the 1860s, actress Pauline Cushman dazzled New York as a genuine Civil War hero and—even more rare for a woman in that era—a spy. Cushman was born Harriet Wood in New Orleans, but changed her name when she took to the stage. While performing in Louisville, Kentucky, she volunteered her services to the Union cause. Posing as a Confederate camp follower through Kentucky and Tennessee, Cushman collected information on Confederate troop movements. After being arrested with sensitive documents in her possession, Cushman was imprisoned and sentenced to death. Her execution was postponed because of her poor health, then canceled in the face of advancing Union troops and the Confederate retreat.

By 1864, Cushman was famous in New York, and President Lincoln bestowed upon her the rank of Brevet

Major, leading many to call her Miss Major Cushman. One night, a crowd of Cushman's admirers gathered outside her ***Astor House Hotel*** residence on ***Broadway between Vesey and Barclay Streets*** ❼ to serenade her with patriotic songs. The *New York Times* gushed:

> *A large number of citizens gathered on the sidewalk in front of the Astor House, about 11 o'clock last evening, to testify their appreciation of the eminent service of Miss Major CUSHMAN, the gallant Union scout and spy, whose daring and skill have elicited the warmest commendations of ROSECRANS, GARFIELD, and other Union officers. A fine band was in attendance and greeted the fair Major with several patriotic airs. Miss CUSHMAN appeared at a window in the second story and was introduced to the assembly by Mr. F.W.B. HIBBARD, Esq., of this City. She was received with three cheers.*

Published in 1865, her biography, titled *Life of Pauline Cushman, the Celebrated Union Spy and Scout: Comprising Her Early History; Her Entry into the Secret Service of the Army of the Cumberland, and Exciting Adventure with the Rebel Chieftains and Others While Within the Enemy's Lines; Together with Her Capture and Sentence to Death by General Bragg and Final Rescue by the Union Army under General Rosecrans,* caused a sensation. The book was written by a friend, Ferdinand Sarmiento. Sarmiento extolled Cushman as:

> *not one of the milk-and-water women of the day, whose only thought is of dress and amusement, but one of the women of old, whose soul was in their country's good. Dashing, charming, fearless, yet lady-like, she combines in herself all the daring of a soldier and all the modesty of the woman.*

"NOT ONE OF THE MILK-AND-WATER WOMEN OF THE DAY, WHOSE ONLY THOUGHT IS OF DRESS . . . BUT ONE . . . WHOSE SOUL WAS IN THEIR COUNTRY'S GOOD.

–Excerpt from biography of Pauline Cushman

WORLD WAR I

During the "war to end all wars" New York became a battleground of espionage, sabotage, and propaganda. Ships steaming out of New York Harbor unknowingly carried explosives concealed within their coalbunkers–sinking vessels "mysteriously" in mid-voyage. Acts of sabotage against factories producing supplies for the Allies were a constant threat, and ambitious propaganda campaigns by both British and German operatives attempted to influence American politicians and public opinion. Colorful, reckless, and courageous are all terms that could apply to New York's World War I spies, operating amid the bustle of crowded city streets, a rapidly expanding skyline of skyscrapers, and technological marvels that were ushering in the new century.

"CODE WAR SPIES"

THE AMERICAN BLACK CHAMBER

141 East 37th Street

America's first code-breaking organization began in 1912 in a now-destroyed townhouse belonging to society figure T. Suffern Tailer, at *3 East 38th Street.* During World War I, it became the Army Cryptographic section of Military Intelligence (MI-8). After the war, the organization was renamed the Cipher Bureau, or Black Chamber, and operated as a joint effort of the State and War Departments. Over time, the operation moved to ***141 East 37th Street,*** ❶ then to *52 Vanderbilt Avenue.* ❷ Operating under a business cover of the Code Computing Company, the firm could be contacted via letter sent to P.O. Box 354, Grand Central Station or by dialing VAnderbilt 7539.

America's first dedicated cryptographic operation was based in New York and headed by code-breaking genius Herbert O. Yardley. The ominous sounding name, Black Chamber, is derived from the 16th-century French term *cabinet noir*—secret facilities where European royalty gathered intelligence from intercepted letters.

"GENTLEMEN DO NOT READ EACH OTHER'S MAIL."

– Secretary of State Henry L. Stimson

Code Computing produced codebooks for secret business communications, including one entitled *Universal Trade Code*, which turned a profit, a rarity for cover companies. Its real business, however, was in breaking the diplomatic communications of other nations. The highly successful code-breaking efforts were led by cryptographer Herbert O. Yardley, who lived on the top floor of the *38th Street* location. Yardley's organization continued until 1929, when Secretary of State Henry L. Stimson famously declared, "Gentlemen do not read each other's mail." Soon afterwards, the State Department and then the Army withdrew the Black Chamber's funding.

Two years later, without government sanction, Yardley published a book-length account of the secret operation called *The American Black Chamber,* revealing many cryptographic successes against foreign governments, most notably Japan. The book made Yardley a celebrity, but official anger at the unauthorized publication of such sensitive information precluded him from future government work. Yardley continued writing and produced a book of puzzles called *Yardleygrams.* A radio drama followed, sponsored by Forhans toothpaste, which offered a vial of secret ink and a decoder to listeners who sent in empty toothpaste boxes. Yardley also wrote fiction, including *The Red Sun of Nippon* and *The Blonde Countess.* The latter became a hit 1935 movie, *Rendezvous,* starring William Powell as the handsome, heroic cryptologist (William Gordon) and Rosalind Russell as his glamorous love interest (Joel Carter).

Stimson's views on the value of cryptanalysis reversed after he became secretary of war during World War II. As secretary, Stimson relied heavily on decrypted enemy communications for wartime policy decisions. America's ability to secretly read "other gentlemen's mail" provided the Allies with a significant advantage that shortened the war.

Yardley died in 1958 and is buried at Arlington National Cemetery. In 1999, 110 years after his birth, he received well-deserved recognition in the Hall of Honor at the National Security Agency, America's present-day code-breaking service.

PROPAGANDA FOR THE KAISER

THE NEW YORK EVENING MAIL

34 Park Row

Originally located at ***34 Park Row,*** 3 the *New York Evening Mail* dated to the 1830s. But the newspaper itself became front-page news in 1918 when publisher Edward A. Rumely was arrested for perjury. The pro-German Rumely purchased the paper in 1915 and soon thereafter changed the editorial policy from anti-Kaiser to pro-German.

However, the funding source for Rumely's acquisition of the paper was suspect and anti-German papers, including the *New York Times*, headlined that the *New York Evening Mail* was part of a massive German propaganda campaign. Rumely was accused of financing the purchase from a $30 million German fund earmarked for influencing the hearts and minds of Americans. Rumely denied the charges but was convicted of violating the Trading with the Enemy Act in 1918. He subsequently received a presidential pardon. The *New York Evening Mail* ceased publication in 1924 following a merger with the *New York Telegram.* Rumely once again emerged as a controversial public figure in the 1930s when he organized protest groups against Roosevelt's New Deal.

THE "BLONDE MATA HARI"

MADAME MARIE DE VICTORICA

541 Washington Street

In the autumn of 1917, MI-8, the Army Cryptographic section of military intelligence, established a laboratory and office in the U.S. postal facility at ***541 Washington Street*** 4 to screen letters for secret writing. The office examined an estimated 2,000 letters a week and in April 1918 identified a major German spy ring led by Herman Wessels, an employee of the Hamburg-Amerika Steamship line. The ring included Madame Marie de Victorica, dubbed the "blonde Mata Hari." The glamorous daughter of a Prussian general, Victorica ultimately stole the headlines.

Born Baroness Maria von Krestschman of "royal blood," the attractive, world-traveling, thirty-eight-year-old "Kin of the Kaiser" had been married multiple times and was addicted to morphine. In New York, she operated from the Waldorf-Astoria Hotel, then at ***Fifth Avenue and 33rd Street***, 5 undercover as a journalist (the Waldorf-Astoria now stands at ***301 Park Avenue***). 6 She secretly corresponded with Berlin using an invisible ink, which was impregnated into one of her scarves before her voyage and reconstituted by soaking the fabric in distilled water.

The original Waldorf-Astoria Hotel stood on the site now occupied by the Empire State Building.

Wessels and the baroness recruited a group from the radical Irish American community to sabotage British and American ships. However, before the sabotage operations could be carried out, Marie de Victorica was arrested at the *Hotel Nassau in Long Beach, N.Y.* Newspapers reported she appeared in court in a sable coat and diamonds, as if dressed for the opera. Despite the evidence against her and Wessels, the two were acquitted. Madame Marie de Victorica, who later cooperated with the U.S. government, remained addicted to morphine and died in a private sanitarium at ***41 East 78th Street*** 7 in 1920.

MT9

GERMANY'S MASTER SABOTEUR

CAPTAIN VON RINTELEN

New York Yacht Club at 37 West 44th Street

World War I German spy Franz von Rintelen

Possibly the most imaginative saboteur of World War I operated in New York City. Captain Franz Dagobert Johannes von Rintelen, a former Deutsche Bank executive and German naval intelligence officer, arrived in New York using a false Swiss passport with the alias Emil V. Gaché (also spelled Emile Gasché) in April 1915. At his disposal was $500,000 ($11 million in current value) to

Von Rintelen called the *beaux-arts*, nautically themed New York Yacht Club clubhouse home while operating in New York. At that time, the birthplace of the America's Cup had only three German members—the Kaiser, his brother, and Rintelen.

disrupt the flow of American munitions to allies. Checking in to the *Great Northern Hotel* (now Le Parker Meridien) at ***118 West 57th Street***, 8 von Rintelen changed his alias to Frederick Hansen and opened an import-export front company on *Cedar Street* under the name E. V. Gibbons. However, it was necessary for him to use his true name at the ***New York Yacht Club at 37 West 44th Street***, 9 where his membership pre-dated the war. Von Rintelen skirted the potential compromise by using the ***German Club at 112 Central Park South*** 10 for his residential address.

Working with a chemist from Hoboken named Dr. Scheele, the pair devised timed explosive devices, using an interned German ship in New York Harbor, the *Friedrich der Grosse*, as a bomb factory. Under international law, the ship was treated similarly to embassies, allowing them to work undisturbed as they turned out dozens of the timed devices. Von Rintelen then recruited dockworkers to plant the bombs in ships' coal bunkers. Numerous ships that sunk in the Atlantic during the time can be attributed to von Rintelen's efforts.

Next, he financed a front organization called Labor's National Peace Council to organize strikes at munitions factories and promote American neutrality. The Labor's National Peace Council operated from offices at ***55 Liberty Street***. 11 Von Rintelen also moved forward with a plot to reinstall ousted Mexican dictator José Victoriano Huerta Márquez, conducting multiple meetings in the ***Ansonia Hotel, 2109 Broadway between 73rd and 74th Streets***. 12 The plot entailed providing the former dictator ten thousand rifles and a large amount of money in exchange for staging a coup in Mexico that would spur Mexico into declaring war against the U.S.

Unfortunately for von Rintelen, his cover unraveled after a few months. His communications were compromised when *Room 40,* the code-breaking section of the British Admiralty, decrypted a telegram to von Rintelen from a colleague and alerted the Americans. The German intelligence officer and saboteur fled the U.S., but was arrested and jailed in England. He returned to the U.S. and received a four-year sentence.

Von Rintelen was also implicated in the 1916 munitions depot explosion at Black Tom Island—a thin peninsula that jutted out into New York Harbor from the New Jersey side. So powerful was the blast, windows in Manhattan were shattered, the Statue of Liberty sustained shrapnel damage, and effects were felt as far away as Maryland. Von Rintelen denied direct involvement in the explosion, but in his 1933 book, *Dark Invader*, he confessed to casing the facility during his time in New York. He died in England in 1949.

"WILD BILL" DONOVAN

FIGHTING 69TH REGIMENTAL ARMORY

68 Lexington Avenue between 25th and 26th Streets

The 69th Regiment Armory is the home to artifacts from the life of General William Donovan, World War I Medal of Honor recipient and World War II head of the Office of Strategic Services.

New York City's only official Irish regiment, the "Fighting 69th" at ***68 Lexington Avenue between 25th and 26th Streets,*** 13 was William "Wild Bill" Donovan's regiment during World War I. Awarded the Medal of Honor for his World War I combat actions, Donovan would later lead the OSS, the World War II forerunner to the Central Intelligence Agency. In 1986, the CIA and the Sixty-Ninth Regiment cosponsored a ceremony and exhibit honoring Donovan's service, *With the Fighting Sixty-Ninth: Donovan in World War I.* Donovan's Medal of

"[DONOVAN'S] THE SORT OF GUY WHO THOUGHT NOTHING OF PARACHUTING INTO FRANCE, BLOWING UP A BRIDGE, PISSING IN LUFTWAFFE GAS TANKS, THEN DANCING ON THE ROOF OF THE ST. REGIS WITH A GERMAN SPY."

– John Ford, Hollywood movie director and OSS officer

"Wild Bill" Donovan

Honor, uniform, footlocker, and other personal items are housed in the armory.

"LAWYERS, GUNS AND MONEY"

MT15 SIDNEY "ACE OF SPIES" REILLY RESIDENCE

Gotham Hotel (now The Peninsula New York), 2 West 55th Street

Born Solomon or Sigmund Rosenblum in Russia, Sidney Reilly has gained the reputation as one of the most colorful and mysterious spies of the twentieth century. Reputed to be fluent in five languages and an avid collector of Napoleana, Reilly likely spied for at least four nations. One observer commented, "He had eleven passports and a wife to go with each one." Some speculate Ian Fleming used Reilly as a model for his fictional spy, James Bond.

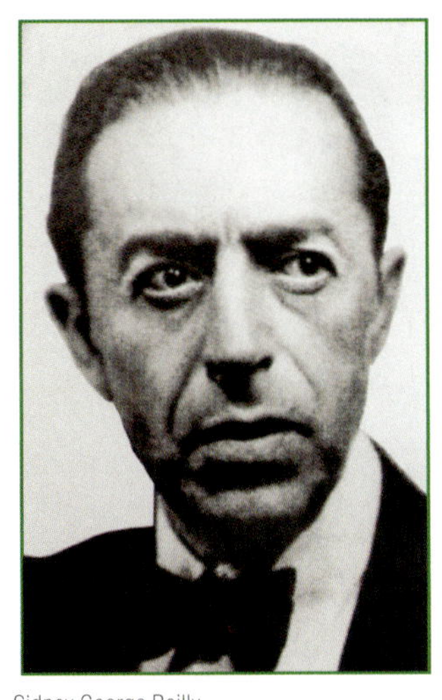

Sidney George Reilly

Before World War I, Reilly was involved in secret operations against Germany, but details of his career remain murky. A healthy portion of his legendary exploits were likely self-created, and even historians who consider him a superspy agree the Reilly legend is inflated.

What can be confirmed is that from 1914 to 1916 Reilly operated out of a New York office on the 27th floor of the ***Equitable Building, 120 Broadway*** **14** as a spy, an arms merchant, and a con man engaged with the Russian Supply Committee in the *Flatiron Building, 175 Fifth Avenue*. His multiple residences included ***The Gotham Hotel,***

2 West 55th Street, (15) *now The Peninsula New York,* and *38 West 59th (Central Park South).* Reilly's "business" involved selling and brokering arms to both the Germans and the Russians while rubbing elbows with New York's financial elites at the Bankers Club. After the U.S. entered the war, Reilly's profitable munitions sales dried up and he looked to rekindle his intelligence operations.

One of New York's grand old hotels, The Peninsula was home to Sidney "The Ace of Spies" Reilly during World War I. At that time, it was called The Gotham.

In March of 1918, Reilly began working with the British Secret Intelligence Service. In the wake of the Russian Revolution, he launched an aggressive anti-Bolshevik campaign to restore the Czar, rescue the Romanov family from imprisonment, and assassinate Vladimir Lenin. He even sold off his beloved Napoleon memorabilia to fund the effort. Many consider this to be Reilly's most daring plot, but on the eve of the coup, unexpected events thwarted the operation. At the end of the war, the British recognized his service. In 1919, Sidney Reilly was awarded the Military Cross "for distinguished services rendered in connection with military operations in the field."

The Ace of Spies met his fate sometime in 1925 after he was lured back into Soviet Russia through Finland by an old nemesis, Felix "Iron Felix" Dzershinsky, the wily chief of the Soviet OGPU. Reilly was ostensibly to meet with an anti-Communist organization operating under the code name OPERATION TRUST and be at the vanguard of a revolution to overthrow the new Soviet government. In reality, TRUST was an elaborate ruse engineered by Dzershinsky to consolidate and eliminate foreign opposition to the new Bolshevik government. After crossing the Finnish border into Russia, the Ace of Spies was captured and interrogated at the OGPU headquarters at Lubyanka Prison in Moscow. Realizing his position was hopeless, Reilly wrote a lengthy confession to Dzershinsky and pled for his life, but to no avail. He was executed in a forest near Moscow on November 5, 1925. His corpse was photographed for documentation as it lay in Lubyanka. After Reilly's death, Soviet guards found his diary hidden in his cell; photographic copies of it, along with his confession, reside in the Russian intelligence archive.

MUNDO NULLA FIDES
(NO FAITH IN THE WORLD)

– Sidney "Ace of Spies" Reilly's Latin motto

PAYMASTER FOR SABOTEURS

G. AMSINCK & COMPANY

6 Hanover Street, downtown Manhattan

THE IDEA WAS TO SPY AS WELL AS DISRUPT THE FLOW OF MUNITIONS AND RAW MATERIALS TO ENGLAND AND FRANCE.

A popular figure in Washington's diplomatic circles, by the outbreak of World War I, Germany's military attaché, Captain Franz von Papen, was busy setting up espionage and sabotage networks in the U.S. Along with his naval attaché, Karl Boy-Ed, the two proved remarkably successful. The idea was to spy as well as disrupt the flow of munitions and raw materials to England and France. Fires broke out in factories, such as the John A. Roebling facility in New Jersey, a steel company instrumental in the Brooklyn Bridge construction decades before. Explosions ripped through gunpowder plants in Delaware, New Jersey, and Pennsylvania. Boats began sinking at sea under suspicious circumstances and at least one train was derailed. The most ambitious plan was to blow up the Welland Canal, connecting Lake Ontario and Lake Erie, stalling the shipments of raw materials from Canada. That plot was foiled by U.S. law enforcement. Behind the scenes, financing a good portion of the destruction, was the trading firm G. Amsinck & Co. at *6 Hanover Street in downtown Manhattan.* 16 Von Papen bought the firm to use its banking division as the unseen paymaster for his intelligence activities and sabotage.

By 1916, the game was up and the U.S. government moved against Amsinck. Officials at the firm responded with a cover story, claiming they cashed only small checks for von Papen because he had no New York bank account. When America entered World War I in 1917, the government stepped in to close the operation by selling Amsinck to American International Corporation and purging the company of German nationals in its top spots. Captain von Papen had long returned to Germany to command a battalion on the Western front. However, he came into the public eye again in 1932 as Germany's Chancellor. He was a major player in bringing Hitler to power by assisting in the dissolution of the Weimar Republic.

EXILED IN THE BRONX

LEON TROTSKY

1522 Vyse Avenue near East 172nd Street

When Leon Trotsky, exiled from Russia and on the run, arrived in New York in early January of 1917, even the hardcore Marxist couldn't contain his enthusiasm for the city. "Here I was in New York, city of prose and fantasy," he wrote in his autobiography, *My Life.* Then, catching himself, he tempered his language with obligatory revolutionary dourness, ". . . of capitalist automatism, its streets a triumph of cubism, its moral philosophy that of the dollar."

Trotsky's family, apparently, was not as committed to the austerity of the Communist cause. "That apartment, at eighteen dollars a month, was equipped with all sorts of conveniences that we Europeans were quite unused to: electric lights, gas cooking-range, bath, telephone, automatic service-elevator, and even a chute for the garbage," he conceded. "These things completely won the boys over to New York."

Exactly where Trotsky lived is still open to debate; he was used to a life of secrecy and never publicized his address. The "workers' district" he described in his book is undoubtedly the Bronx, but does not mention a precise address. The best–though still disputed–location is ***1522 Vyse Avenue near East 172nd Street.*** 17 Another possibility is somewhere along *Prospect Avenue south of 186th Street.*

This Vyse Avenue address in the Bronx is a likely residence of Leon Trotsky during his brief stay in New York. While the precise address of the Russian revolutionary is disputed, Trotsky vividly recalled the exact amount of his rent in his memoirs–$18.00 a month.

More certain is where Trotsky worked. Despite a heavy lecture schedule, he wrote for the paper *Novy Mir* (*New World*), located at ***77 St. Marks Place*** **18** in the East Village. Within a few weeks of Trotsky's arrival in New York, the Bolshevik Revolution overthrew Tsar Nicholas II and Trotsky sailed for Russia. *The Bronx Home News* reported the local angle with somewhat outsized borough pride, proclaiming in a headline, BRONX MAN LEADS RUSSIAN REVOLUTION.

Leon Trotsky found employment during his few weeks in New York writing for the revolutionary paper, *Novy Mir* (*New World*) on St. Marks Place. The building still stands.

From Moscow, Trotsky rebuilt the Red Army, engineered a victory in the Russian Civil War, and became the second most powerful man in Russia after Vladimir Lenin. Ultimately, however, he was politically out-maneuvered by archrival Joseph Stalin and was exiled again in 1928. Twelve years later, New York City was the operational base for a Soviet assassination plot that ended the exiled Trotsky's life outside Mexico City.

SPY AND PLAYWRIGHT

LM19 SIR WILLIAM WISEMAN, 10th BARONET

44 Whitehall Street

Sir William George Eden Wiseman, 10th Baronet, had a biography as colorful as his name. A graduate of Cambridge, he was a boxer, playwright, and journalist before turning his attention to banking, a profession interrupted by World War I. After surviving a combat gas attack at Flanders, he was recruited into the War Office section of Britain's MI6, called MIIc. Arriving in New York City with a companion in the fall of 1915, the two identified themselves as "merchants," giving their local business address as the accounting firm of Touche & Niven (a predecessor of accounting firm Deloitte Touche Tohmatsu

Limited) at *30 Broad Street*. Soon, however, Wiseman was installed in the British Consulate at ***44 Whitehall Street*** **19** in Lower Manhattan as a low-level functionary in the Purchasing Commission of the British Ministry of Munitions. He eventually took over intelligence operations targeting German American organizations and anti-British Indian and Irish groups from Australian Captain Sir Guy Gaunt.

Woodrow Wilson

Wiseman moved into the luxury **Gotham Hotel, now the Peninsula New York at *2 West 55th Street*** **15** that was also the residence of Colonel Edward Mandel House, a trusted advisor to President Woodrow Wilson. Together, the pair acted as conduits of unofficial diplomacy between Great Britain and the president. Also living at the hotel was Sidney "Ace of Spies" Reilly, the spy and arms merchant.

Sir William Wiseman

With World War I raging in Europe and America still neutral, Wiseman and his network attempted to discredit the Germans while urging America to enter the fray. In one of his operations, Wiseman arranged for pictures of the German Ambassador, Count J. H. von Bernstorff, cavorting with two women (neither his wife) to appear in the nation's newspapers.

After the war, Wiseman remained in New York City, working for the investment house of Kuhn, Loeb & Co. while dabbling in the theater as a playwright and launching a play called *Her Lord and Master* in 1929. In 1939, he was called back to duty to help William Stephenson set up the British Security Coordination (BSC), modeled, in large part, on his original intelligence operation.

GERMANY'S BOND GIRL

DESPINA STORCH

Mount Olivet Cemetery, 6504 Grand Avenue, Maspeth, Queens

Despina Storch

She was beautiful, mysterious, and a spy. Born in Turkey, Despina Storch married when she was just seventeen, but divorced not long after. Whether she entered the spy game through her ex-husband or some other way remains a mystery, but there is no doubt of her profession. Living under a string of aliases, including Madame Nezie, Madame Hesketh, and Madame Davidovitch, among others, she crisscrossed Europe. Accompanied by Baron Henri de Beville, Storch sought out military and diplomatic contacts at parties and other social events. By the time they reached New York, the pair had attracted another couple, a German woman, Elizabeth Charlotte Nix, and Robert de Clarmont, who may or may not have been a French count. They initially checked into the Biltmore Hotel at *335 Madison Avenue* (now the Bank of America Plaza) and then moved to the original ***Waldorf-Astoria at 33rd Street and Fifth Avenue,*** **5** where the *Empire State Building* now stands.

The four were welcomed at fashionable society events, but authorities became suspicious of their activities. An investigation discovered unexplained large sums of money, bogus passports, coded correspondence, and a safe deposit box with additional coded letters. When Storch was identified as a spy by the French intelligence service, the four were ordered out of the U.S. amid public speculation about firing squads in France. While being held at Ellis Island to await deportation, Storch became ill and died of pneumonia on March 30, 1918, at the age of 23. Rumors accompanied her death. Some said she took her own life with a suicide pill, while others blamed cunning German assassins. She was buried in ***Mount Olivet Cemetery at 6504 Grand Avenue, Maspeth, Queens.*** **20**

BETWEEN
WORLD WARS

Throughout the Jazz Age of the Roaring Twenties and the Depression-era 1930s, Russia's newly formed Communist regime seemed an attractive ideological alternative to critics of capitalism. As Communist and Socialist adherents gained prominence in New York, Stalin's intelligence apparatus rapidly expanded its activities by sending skilled operatives to provoke, incite, and exploit the intellectual and working class followers of Communism. In addition to recruiting spies, Soviet intelligence officers operating in New York stole American technology, ran espionage networks, and even conducted assassinations. Throughout the 1930s, the Soviet NVKD laid the clandestine groundwork in New York for a permanent espionage presence in the United States.

REVOLUTION IN NEW YORK

THE SOCIALIST WORKERS PARTY

Headquarters, 116 University Place

The Socialist Workers Party (SWP), loyal to Leon Trotsky, established its headquarters at ***116 University Place.*** 1 Led by James P. Cannon, code name DAK, party members were devout followers of the exiled Trotsky, code name OLD MAN, and his Fourth International—they were mortal enemies of the Stalinists. Unknowingly, however, they were thoroughly infiltrated by Stalinist agents, including Cannon's secretary, Sylvia Caldwell, code names SATYR and RITA. Caldwell reported on all correspondence between the exiled Trotsky and Cannon, with SWP information ultimately playing a role in the plot to assassinate Trotsky.

Near Union Square, the epicenter for New York's early-20th-century political radicals, the Socialists Workers Party and the rival Communist Party USA headquarters were within walking distance of each other. The SWP's building is now the site of a deli and apartments.

THE NAÏVE ASSASSIN

ROBERT SHELDON HARTE

Residence, 1148 Fifth Avenue

The SWP undertook an important role in fundraising to support Leon Trotsky's life in exile and provided a small contingent of American bodyguards to protect him at his compound in Coyoacan, Mexico. One of these guards, who lived at ***1148 Fifth Avenue,*** a was Robert Sheldon Harte, the son of wealthy businessman Jesse S. Harte. Unknown to Trotsky, Harte was secretly an agent for Stalin, recruited by Iosif Grigulevich, a legendary Soviet intelligence officer, code name AMUR or CUPID. Harte, on guard duty in Coyoacan on the night of May 23, 1940, allowed a group of two dozen attackers dressed as Mexican

Raised in a Fifth Avenue apartment, Robert Sheldon Harte joined radical politics at an early age. The naïve New Yorker conspired with Stalin-directed assassins, not understanding their lethal intent toward Trotsky.

policemen to enter the Trotsky compound and storm his living quarters. The assassins, led by Grigulevich, code name PADRE, included Mexican muralist David Alfaro Siqueiros, code name KON, and Luis Arenal, code name RAFAIL. The attackers fired hundreds of rounds into Trotsky's bedroom and living quarters, but, miraculously, he survived the attack unscathed.

THE ATTACKERS FIRED HUNDREDS OF ROUNDS INTO TROTSKY'S BEDROOM AND LIVING QUARTERS, BUT, MIRACULOUSLY, HE SURVIVED THE ATTACK UNSCATHED.

Efforts by the American SWP to raise funds to strengthen the defenses of his compound after the attack were woefully inadequate, as Trotsky's trustful nature and refusal to permit his guards to search guests prevailed over stronger security measures. Trotsky's misguided sense of civility contributed to his death less than three months later at the hands of an ice-axe-wielding assassin.

TROTSKY'S ATTACKERS IN HIDING

NEW YORK CITY SAFE HOUSE

881 Washington Avenue, Brooklyn

Following the May 23, 1940, attack on Trotsky's compound in Coyoacan, Mexico, Robert Sheldon Harte, the guard on duty, appeared to leave willingly with the failed assassins in Trotsky's two vehicles—he was never seen alive again. His father rushed to Mexico from New York City to search for his son, only to discover decaying remains a month later buried beneath the kitchen of a remote safe house used by the attackers. Trotsky refused to believe Harte betrayed him and commissioned a commemorative plaque erected near the guard post in his honor. A search of Harte's

A commemorative plaque for Robert Sheldon Harte is posted on the gatehouse of Leon Trotsky's compound in Coyoacan, Mexico.

room in his father's New York City residence, however, revealed a different story—a large painting of Joseph Stalin, Trotsky's rival, was displayed on the son's wall.

Later accounts revealed that Leopolo Arenal, code name ALEXANDER, and his brother, Luis, both hardened veterans of the Mexican Brigade of the Spanish Civil War, killed and buried Harte when they feared he would go to the authorities and confess his role. Grigulevich, who recruited the naive Harte, had led him to believe the attack was intended only to destroy Trotsky's archive, not to assassinate him.

Luis fled Mexico after Harte's body was discovered and resided secretly with his wife, Rose Arenal, at ***881 Washington Avenue, Brooklyn***. 3 Rose later admitted to the FBI that she acted as a mail drop for the brothers; the messages were picked up by American Elizabeth Bentley, a recruited Soviet agent, code name CLEVER GIRL.

This quiet apartment building at 881 Washington Avenue, not far from the Brooklyn Botanic Gardens, served as a safe house for Luis Arenal and his wife, Rose, after the botched attempt on Trotsky's life.

PLOTTING TROTSKY'S DEATH

HOTEL PIERREPONT

55 Pierrepont Street, between Henry and Hicks Streets, Brooklyn Heights

Room 737 of the unassuming Hotel Pierrepont at ***55 Pierrepont Street, between Henry and Hicks Streets in Brooklyn Heights*** 4 served as a $15-a-week safe house in 1940 for Soviet agent Ramon Mercader, code name RAYMOND and later GNOME, who operated under the aliases Jacques Mornard and Frank Jacson. Following the failed nighttime raid on Trotsky's Mexican compound on May 23,

Built in 1928, the Hotel Pierrepont—a stone's throw from downtown Brooklyn—was the temporary headquarters for Trotsky assassin Ramon Mercader.

1940, Mercader returned to New York City to meet with his mother, Caridad. Code named MOTHER and KLAVA, Caridad acted as the operational controller for the next attack. In Mercader's hotel room, the plan to kill Trotsky was finalized with the support and guidance of the chief NKVD intelligence officer in the U.S., Gaik Ovakimian, code name GENNADI.

Mercader's access to Trotsky was through an unwitting New York Trotskyite, Sylvia Ageloff. From June 14 to 30, 1940, Mercader, registered under the name Jacson, stayed with his "wife," Ageloff, in room 737 at the Pierrepont, but left New York without her to return to Mexico City. Still unwitting, and believing her lover to be apolitical, Ageloff joined him later that summer.

Familiar to the Trotsky guards and trusted because of his affair with Ageloff, Mercader inveigled his way into the compound and met Trotsky on multiple occasions during July and August of 1940. He became the only person ever allowed to meet alone with the exiled revolutionary. On the afternoon of August 20, 1940, Mercader struck Trotsky from behind with a shortened ice-climbing axe, delivering a fatal blow to the right side of his head. Trotsky did not die instantly, as was the plan, and let out a mortal scream. Guards in the next room quickly overwhelmed Mercader.

A block away, the overall planner of the assassination, Leonoid Eitingon, code name TOM and PIERRE, surveilled the events through binoculars. Mercader's mother, Caridad, was waiting outside the compound in a taxi to rush him to a nearby airfield where a chartered aircraft would fly them to Cuba. However, with Mercader now captured, Caridad and Eitingon, who were also lovers, escaped Mexico by ship, eventually reaching Moscow, where they were handsomely rewarded.

The jailed Mercader never admitted his true identity during years of interrogation. He served twenty years in a Mexican prison before his release in 1960. Honored as a hero of the Soviet Union, the solid gold watch he was awarded in 1965 by the Central Committee was inscribed to him with a previously unknown code name, AGENT LOPEZ.

By the 1970s, the *Hotel Pierrepont* had deteriorated so much it might have scared off even a professional assassin like Mercader. Today, the rehabilitated site is the St. Charles Jubilee Senior Center of Brooklyn.

EDITOR BY DAY, SPY BY NIGHT

THE DAILY WORKER NEWSPAPER

35 East 12th Street

The *Daily Worker* newspaper at ***35 East 12th Street*** (5), published by the Central Committee of the Communist Party U.S.A. (CPUSA), began operation in 1924 and reached a peak circulation of 35,000 during the 1930s. Louis Budenz held a number of positions at the *Daily Worker* and, prior to 1938, had been arrested more than twenty times for his activist politics. With these qualifications, he was eventually promoted to editor of the *Daily Worker* and granted membership on the prestigious National Committee of the CPUSA.

This 1897 building boasts multimillion-dollar loft apartments with 12-foot ceilings and gourmet kitchens. In earlier years, it was headquarters for the radical *Daily Worker* newspaper, published by the Communist Party U.S.A.

Lesser known was the active role Budenz played as a Soviet agent, code names BUBEN and TAMBOURINE, and head of a group of six spies. In 1945, Budenz renounced Communism and appeared as an expert witness at government hearings. He also offered a series of books on his life as a Communist. Among his revelations to the FBI was his role in recruiting Ruby Weil, a member of the American Workers Party, to facilitate the introduction of Trotskyite Sylvia Ageloff to eventual Trotsky assassin Ramon Mercader (aka Jacques Mornard and Frank Jacson) at a secret meeting in Paris in 1938.

The Ageloff-Mercader relationship was the essential element in the plot to infiltrate Mercader into the Trotsky compound in Coyoacan, Mexico. Soon after Weil engineered the introduction, Ageloff and

SOVIET INTELLIGENCE LAID THE GROUNDWORK FOR WHAT WOULD LATER BECOME ITS MOST SUCCESSFUL OPERATION, THE THEFT OF THE PLANS FOR THE ATOMIC BOMB.

Mercader became lovers and Weil returned to the U.S. Years after the assassination, Weil, as well as Budenz, claimed they never understood the true purpose of the Ageloff-Mercader introduction. Both maintained they were told it was part of a plan to save Stalin's life.

"COMMUNISM IS 20TH-CENTURY AMERICANISM."

- Earl Browder

TALENT SPOTTING FOR SPIES

COMMUNIST PARTY HEADQUARTERS

35 East 12th Street

New York's *Union Square* and its surrounding neighborhood was a hotbed of radical politics and Communist protests in the decade before World War II. The Socialist Workers Party (SWP), loyal to Leon Trotsky, established its headquarters at *116 University Place*, while the Stalinist-led Communist Party of the United States of America (CPUSA) was housed at ***35 East 12th Street.*** 5 The two organizations attracted tens of thousands to rallies during the Great Depression, where protesters heard native Kansan Earl Browder, head of the American Communist Party, proclaim, "Communism is 20th-Century Americanism." No one knew that Browder was a Soviet agent, with the code name FATHER.

Both organizations were hunting grounds for Soviet intelligence officers to spot ideologically motivated individuals who could be recruited as spies. For example, Flora Wovschin, code name ZORA, became an active recruiter for Soviet intelligence and drew Judith Coplon, code name SIMA, from Barnard College into espionage. Elizabeth Bentley, code name CLEVER GIRL, was recruited in much the same manner after completing her masters at Columbia University. So successful was the Soviet intelligence apparatus in the 1930s that by the time the United States entered WW II, the U.S. government was penetrated at multiple levels. Soviet intelligence laid the groundwork for what would later become its most successful operation, the theft of the plans for the atomic bomb.

The CPUSA's long-time headquarters on *East 12th Street* has since been converted to multimillion-dollar lofts and the organization has moved to ***235 West 23rd Street.*** 6

SPY CENTRAL IN TIMES SQUARE AREA

HOTEL TAFT

Seventh Avenue between West 50th and 51st Streets

If you were a newly arrived Russian spy in New York in the 1930s, chances are good you stayed at the ***Hotel Taft,*** now the *Michelangelo*, on ***Seventh Avenue between 50th and 51st Streets.*** 7 If your contact at the hotel welcomed you with a *parole* such as, "Greetings from Fanny," the required answer would be, "Thank you. How is she?"

First opened in 1926 as the Manger Hotel and renamed for President Taft in 1931, this enormous Times Square hotel was the hostelry of choice for visiting spies. Today, the hotel, called the Michelangelo, also features hundreds of condominiums.

Throughout the years, the Taft provided rooms for an assortment of spies, including notable Soviet operative Valentin Markin and German Captain Ulrich von der Osten, an *Abwehr* intelligence officer operating under deep cover as a Spanish national. When the Soviet atomic spy Klaus Fuchs arrived in New York in 1943, he checked into the Hotel Taft before relocating to the Barbizon-Plaza Hotel (now the *Trump Parc East)* at *106 Central Park South.*

Built in 1926 as the Manger, it was renamed for President Taft in 1931. The largest hotel in the Times Square area, the Taft was known for its direct walkway into the lavish Roxy Theatre, called "the Cathedral of the Motion Picture," and the Taft Grill. Today, the majority of its rooms have been converted to condominiums. The Roxy Theatre was demolished in 1960 to make way for an office building.

BATHHOUSE DEATH OF A RUSSIAN SPY

VALENTIN MARKIN

Luxor Baths, 121 West 46th Street

In 1933, Valentin Markin of the Soviet intelligence organization OGPU set up the first illegal residency—called a *rezidentura*—to run spy operations in the U.S. As head of the residency, Markin handled agents while operating under a variety of code names, including ARTHUR, WALTER, OSKAR, HOWARD, and DAVIS. Markin's death, however, is even more mysterious than his secret intelligence work in New York. In August of 1934, he appeared at the now defunct ***Luxor Baths, 121 West 46th Street,*** 8 with a large gash on his forehead. Rushed to a nearby hospital, Markin gave the story that he had been in a taxi accident. He died a few days later without revealing any other details.

Unsubstantiated stories about his death soon circulated. One asserted Markin was murdered on Stalin's orders for being a Trotskyite. His wife, back in the Soviet Union, was told her husband was killed by "American gangsters." Another tale had Markin mugged leaving a midtown speakeasy. Still another put the blame on fellow Soviet intelligence officers seeking revenge for a memo he wrote criticizing colleagues.

Markin left behind an American girlfriend, a business partner who held a cover job at a cosmetics company that was privy to intelligence secrets, and a bank safe-deposit box containing sensitive documents. The full story has never been revealed, but the intelligence efforts begun by Markin in the 1930s have continued in New York City and the U.S. without interruption.

THE FULL STORY HAS NEVER BEEN REVEALED, BUT THE INTELLIGENCE EFFORTS BEGUN BY MARKIN IN THE 1930S HAVE CONTINUED IN NEW YORK CITY AND THE U.S. WITHOUT INTERRUPTION.

Where the elite once met to sweat, the Luxor Baths are now a historical memory.

THE LUXOR BATHS WAS A CELEBRITY STEAM ROOM THAT HOSTED NOTABLES LIKE JACKIE GLEASON AND JACK DEMPSEY.

THE VANISHING SPY

JULIET STUART POYNTZ

American Women's Association,
353 West 57th Street

A founding member of the Communist Party of the United States(CPUSA), Juliet Stuart Poyntz mysteriously disappeared after she threatened to expose Stalin's purges in the Soviet Union.

On June 3, 1937, Juliet Stuart Poyntz left her room at what was then the American Women's Association Clubhouse (formerly the Henry Hudson Hotel and now the Hudson Hotel) at *353 West 57th Street* 9 and vanished. A police investigation into her fate turned up no clues. All her belongings, clothing, and hand luggage were left untouched in the room. Even a page of writing was left uncompleted on the desk. Poyntz, who taught at Columbia University and Barnard, was a founding member of the American Communist Party and once considered one of the top ten Communist leaders in the United States. She began as a progressive activist who drifted increasingly into Communism. Poyntz is believed to have publicly withdrawn from the Communist Party in 1934 to work underground as an agent for the Soviet GRU (military intelligence). However, a trip to Stalin's Russia in 1936 apparently reversed her views. Returning to New York disillusioned, she spoke openly of plans to write a book exposing the Stalin purges.

ALL HER BELONGINGS, CLOTHING, AND HAND LUGGAGE WERE LEFT UNTOUCHED IN THE ROOM. EVEN A PAGE OF WRITING WAS LEFT UNCOMPLETED ON THE DESK.

Along with news of her disappearance swirled unsubstantiated rumors about the circumstances and the identities of those involved. Poyntz is believed by multiple sources to have been abducted and murdered by an NKVD assassination squad to prevent her defection. One theory holds that she was lured to Central Park at night by a former lover, Shachno Epstein, editor of the Communist Yiddish daily *Freiheit* and an OGPU/NKVD agent. The story is that Epstein led the unsuspecting Poyntz along a side path, where a large, black limousine hugged the edge of the wall in waiting. Two men jumped out, pushed her inside, and sped away to the woods near the Roosevelt family estate in Duchess County. There, they killed Poyntz and buried her body.

Another disillusioned Communist Party member, Benjamin Gitlow, described the abduction and murder in his book, *The Whole of Their Lives: Communism in America.* "The body was covered with lime and dirt. On top were placed dead leaves and branches which the three killers trampled down with their feet." Poyntz's mysterious disappearance was used as a not-so-subtle warning to other party members should they ever consider defecting. The mystery has never been solved. In October 1944, the courts officially declared Poyntz deceased and turned her estate over to her sister.

SLEEPING WITH MANY ENEMIES

MARTHA DODD

The Majestic, 115 Central Park West between 71st and 72nd Streets

The daughter of American Ambassador William E. Dodd, Martha Dodd arrived in Germany in the early 1930s and began a series of affairs with German officers, including General Udet, senior officer of the German air force, and Ernst Hanfstaengl, an aide to Adolf Hitler. Hanfstaengl tried, unsuccessfully, to promote an unlikely romantic liaison between Dodd and Hitler. Dodd then began a passionate affair with Russian Boris Vinogradov, an NKVD officer under Soviet Embassy cover as a press attaché. Moscow Centre encouraged Vinogradov to pursue the romantic relationship and gave Dodd the code name LIZA. The affair paid off. Dodd informed the Soviets of secret embassy business and provided details of her father's official reports to the State Department. The couple eventually separated when Dodd returned to the U.S. Vinogradov was recalled to Moscow, where he was caught up in Stalin's purges and executed.

Known as an "art deco masterpiece," The Majestic features Central Park views at one of Manhattan's most fashionable addresses. The 1930s-era luxury apartment building fit the status and lifestyle of a young, well-off couple like Martha Dodd and Alfred Stern.

Back in New York, Dodd married a wealthy stockbroker, Alfred Stern. The couple took up residence in a penthouse in ***The Majestic, 115 Central Park West between 71st and 72nd Streets,*** (10) where they threw lavish parties and dabbled in liberal politics. The NKVD, however, had not forgotten about their potentially valuable agent. On one hand, they saw Dodd as "gifted and clever," but they also realized she "needed constant control over her behavior." Additionally, the Centre viewed her with disdain as "a typical representative of American bohemia, a sexually decayed woman ready to sleep with any handsome man." Dodd wanted to bring her husband into the ring and, with Centre's approval, found Stern a willing participant. Through their publishing house, the couple provided a business cover to support functions of the Soviet espionage apparatus. They also acted as occasional "spotters" for potential recruits and maintained a substantial bank account for laundering money through front companies.

Called before the Senate Sub-Committee on Un-American Activities in 1956, Dodd and her husband fled the U.S., eventually turning up in Mexico, Prague, Cuba, and Moscow. Martha Dodd died in Prague in 1990.

SOVIET MASTER SPY AND CAPITALIST

ITZHAK AKHMEROV

Henry Bookman Inc., millinery at 19 West 57th Street

Itzhak Akhmerov alias Michael Adamec

Itzhak Akhmerov first arrived in the U.S. in the 1930s, with the code name MER. He operated as a Soviet illegal in New York under the identity Michael Adamec. To backstop his identity, documentation to support the cover was covertly slipped into Cook County, Illinois, birth records. Akhmerov used layers of cutouts between himself and his agents, who knew him only as Mr. Adamec. At some point, he left his Russian wife and married American Helen Lowery, code names NELLY and MADLEN, the niece of Earl Browder, the head of the American Communist Party. Browder was himself a Soviet agent with the code name FATHER.

Living in ***Upper Manhattan at 115 Cabrini Boulevard,*** 11 Akhmerov operated under the cover of a hat shop, ***Henry Bookman, Inc. at 19 West 57th Street,*** 12 while his wife worked as the bookkeeper. Together, the two Communists made Bookman, Inc. a profitable venture. Inspired by this commercial success, Akhmerov proposed a more prominent venture, a furrier shop, to his Moscow bosses. Moscow rejected this New York plan, but later assigned Akhmerov and his dreams to Baltimore, where he opened a furrier shop that operated as a safe house and handled agents such as Elizabeth Bentley and Michael Straight.

ON THE RUN FROM STALIN

WALTER KRIVITSKY'S APARTMENT

36 West Gun Hill Road, The Bronx

After defecting to the West to avoid Stalin's purges, Soviet intelligence officer Major General Walter Krivitsky and his family moved into this apartment house in the Bronx.

The first high-ranking Soviet intelligence officer to defect to the West was Walter Krivitsky, code name ENEMY. An illegal officer of the NKVD and GRU, he walked into a French ministry in Paris with his wife and young child in 1937 rather than return to the Soviet Union and Stalin's purges. He re-emerged in New York, living in an apartment at *36 West Gun Hill Road in The Bronx* 13 in 1939. His book, *In Stalin's Secret Service,* featured his own story along with a vivid account of the murderous Stalin regime. Further, Krivitsky's information enabled Western intelligence agencies to identify scores of GRU and NKVD agents around the world. In December 1941, Krivitsky checked into a room at the Bellevue Hotel in Washington, D.C., at 15 East Street NW, where the maid found him dead with a single gunshot wound to the head the next day. Although officially ruled a suicide, suspicions continue that Stalin ordered a hit on the defector. "Anyone can commit a murder, but it takes an artist to commit a suicide," former Communist Party member Whittaker Chambers quipped at the time.

"ANYONE CAN COMMIT A MURDER, BUT IT TAKES AN ARTIST TO COMMIT A SUICIDE."

– Former Communist Party member Whittaker Chambers

CODE NAME CROOK

CONGRESSMAN SAMUEL DICKSTEIN

Burial Site, Union Field Cemetery, 82-11 Cypress Avenue, Ridgewood, Queens

U.S. Representative Samuel Dickstein was on the Soviet NKVD payroll from 1937 to 1940 under the code name CROOK. The congressman must have seemed like a prize asset, sitting in the center of American political power and spearheading an antifascist investigative subcommittee. Dickstein, who promised to deliver material on the fascist supporters, German agents, and White Russians to his NKVD handler, received $1,250 a month payment for his services.

HIS INTELLIGENCE EFFORTS ATTRACTED NO SUSPICION AND WERE NOT MADE PUBLIC UNTIL DISCOVERED IN THE ARCHIVES IN MOSCOW IN THE EARLY 1990S.

How much useful intelligence the congressman actually provided to the Soviets is uncertain. Responding to inquiries about Soviet defector Walter Krivitsky, Dickstein delivered only a short memo that read suspiciously close to the defector's public statements in the media, though he did sponsor legislation to have Krivitsky deported. In another episode, Dickstein gave a speech requesting more funding for J. Edgar Hoover's FBI, which was then gearing up to fight Soviet spies. Ironically, the antifascist subcommittee Dickstein helped form eventually turned its focus to Communists as the Special Committee on Un-American Activities.

Dickstein resigned from Congress in 1945, after more than twenty years in office. He then served as a judge on the New York State Supreme Court. His intelligence efforts attracted no suspicion and were not made public until discovered in the archives in Moscow in the early 1990s. Dickstein died in 1954 and is buried in the *Union Field Cemetery, 82-11 Cypress Avenue, Ridgewood, Queens.* 14

RUSSIA'S THOMAS EDISON

PROFESSOR LEV SERGEYEVICH THEREMIN

Residence at 37 West 54th Street

Born into Czarist Russia, Lev Theremin gained early recognition as a musical prodigy who performed for Lenin before growing into an inventor with a flair for physics. His genius was co-opted by the Soviet intelligence services, and for nearly ten years, beginning in the late 1920s, Theremin lived in a New York brownstone at *37 West 54th Street.* 15 There, he established Teletouch Corporation (later Teletouch Industries) and promoted a new musical instrument that bore his name, the theremin. The revolutionary electronic device created a sensation in a city always eager for the new and avant-garde.

Russian musical genius, inventor, and Stalin spy, Lev Theremin worked in this midtown townhouse for most of the 1930s. Recalled to Russia by Stalin at the beginning of World War II, Theremin's engineering talents were directed at creating innovative spy devices for the KGB.

The Teletouch Corporation also patented technology that activated advertising devices when shoppers entered an electronic field, and developed the first passive burglar alarm system. Secretly, however, Theremin's primary work was to collect information on American technology for Soviet military intelligence.

Recalled to Moscow in 1938 during the Stalin purges, Theremin's loyalty was questioned simply because he had lived in the West. He was imprisoned and eventually consigned to a *sharashka*, prison laboratory, where he turned out sophisticated covert listening devices for the Soviet intelligence service. Among the most notable of these devices was an audio bug, the *passive cavity resonator*. Concealed in a three-foot-diameter wooden replica of the Great Seal of the United States, the bug was presented to the U.S. ambassador in Moscow as a token of friendship in 1945 by a group of young Russian Pioneers (the Soviet version of the Boy Scouts). The Seal hung above the ambassador's desk, and the device operated undetected until 1952. After the bug was discovered, frustrated CIA engineers unsuccessfully attempted to duplicate the technical functionality of the sophisticated device, which they named "the Thing" as in "How does 'the thing' work?"

Theremin's passive cavity resonator made a dramatic and unanticipated public appearance in New York City at the United Nations in May, 1960, when U.S. Ambassador Henry Cabot Lodge used it to defuse Soviet diplomatic outrage after Gary Powers in a U-2 spy plane was shot down over Russia. For his secret efforts, Theremin never gained public recognition, but he was privately awarded the prestigious Stalin Prize, First Class. He continued his technical work for Soviet intelligence throughout the remainder of his career. Theremin died in Moscow in 1993.

THEREMIN'S LOYALTY WAS QUESTIONED SIMPLY BECAUSE HE HAD LIVED IN THE WEST.

SPIES WITH HARBOR VIEWS

GERMAN CONSULATE

Whitehall Building at 17 Battery Place

Before America's entrance into World War II, the German consulate and International Commercial Agency operated an espionage hub from the 19th floor of the ***Whitehall Building, 17 Battery Place,*** 16 a location known for its spectacular harbor views. Run by Nazi party member Ernst Hopf, the consulate was mysteriously bombed in 1940, but sustained only minimal damage. The attackers were never identified.

A short time later, the building's furnace operator, Walter Morrissey, was ordered to burn official-looking papers. Instead, he smuggled the documents out of the building to the FBI. Those documents would later provide vital evidence in the Ludwig spy ring case. The consulate was closed in late 1941 when America entered the war.

The Whitehall Building in the Battery Park district once harbored German spies.

THE FBI'S DOUBLE AGENT

WILLIAM SEBOLD

Knickerbocker Hotel, 42nd Street and Broadway

Reputed (and disputed) to be the birthplace of the martini, the Knickerbocker Hotel was built by John Jacob Astor IV in 1906. In addition to playing host to celebrities like Enrico Caruso and George M. Cohan, the FBI staged one of its most successful World War II counterintelligence operations at the site.

In the late 1930s, William Sebold held a good job as a mechanic at a California company, Consolidated Aircraft. The native German, born Wilhelm Georg Debrowski, fought in WWI as a machine gunner but later jumped ship in Galveston, Texas, changed his name, married, and became a naturalized U.S. citizen. On a visit to Germany in the summer of 1939, Sebold's life took an unexpected turn when he was approached by German intelligence to spy on America. After agreeing to do so, Sebold reported the "recruitment" to the American consulate in Hamburg.

The Nazis trained Sebold in espionage and sent him back to the U.S. with the alias Harry Sawyer and cover as an engineering consultant. Met at the docks by the FBI on February 8, 1940, Sebold reaffirmed his loyalty to the U.S. and ultimately became one of America's most valuable double agents.

Acting on German instructions to handle communications for an existing group, the Duquesne spy ring, Sawyer (Sebold) set up a front company in the ***Knickerbocker Hotel at 42nd Street and Broadway***, 17 which the FBI wired with microphones and movie cameras. Over the next eighteen months, the double agent made hundreds

HIS MISSION COMPLETE, SEBOLD RECEIVED A NEW IDENTITY FROM THE U.S. GOVERNMENT IN AN EARLY VERSION OF THE WITNESS RELOCATION PROGRAM AND WAS MOVED TO AN UNDISCLOSED LOCATION. HE IS REPORTED TO HAVE DIED IN CALIFORNIA IN 1970.

of shortwave radio transmissions from a site on Long Island, using the call number CQDXVW-Z. The FBI-controlled radio station transmitted 300 messages to Germany and received more than 200 replies. Through Sebold, the FBI identified dozens of German agents in the U.S., Mexico, and South America. When they eventually moved against the German network, more than thirty German spies were arrested and convicted in a trial that concluded less than a week after the bombing of Pearl Harbor. His mission complete, Sebold received a new identity from the U.S. government in an early version of the witness relocation program and was moved to an undisclosed location. He is reported to have died in California in 1970.

A "CRIMINALLY INSANE" SPY

FREDERICK JOUBERT DUQUESNE

Residence, 24 West 76th Street

One of the major spies apprehended by Sebold's operation was Hermann Lang, who had smuggled the Norden Bomb Site plans and mechanism, which enabled all-weather targeting, out of the Carl L. Norden plant at *80 Lafayette Street* (now Lafayette Hall, a New York University dormitory). Another was the owner of the ***Little Casino Bar Restaurant at 206 East 85th Street,*** 18 which served as a meeting place for Nazi spies.

The ring's leader, Frederick Joubert Duquesne, lived under the alias Dunn at ***24 West 76th Street*** 19 and worked at ***Air Terminal Associates at 120 Wall Street.*** 20 Duquesne was a South African adventurer and mercenary who had harbored a pathological hatred

South African-born German spy Frederick Joubert Duquesne lived at this stately Upper West Side townhouse with his accomplice and lover, Evelyn Clayton Lewis, a well-to-do writer and artist from Fayetteville, Arkansas.

of the British since the Boer War. Alleged to have blown up British ships, Duquesne had been in police custody at Bellevue Hospital in New York in 1919. While there, he described himself as a "British prisoner of war, confidential emissary of King Leopold II in the Belgian Congo, big-game hunting instructor to Theodore Roosevelt, reporter, author, publicity man, inventor, and inmate of a hospital for the criminally insane."

Duquesne was also apparently a convincing performer. During his stay at Bellevue, he faked paralysis for two years before escaping by climbing over the hospital wall dressed as a woman. He managed to remain at large for the next two decades, until he was trapped in the Sebold operation. Convicted and jailed, Duquesne served twelve years in prison before dying in 1956 in a charity ward on Welfare Island, now *Roosevelt Island*.

SPIES AND LIES IN NEW YORK CITY

SPYING FOR BRITISH SECURITY COORDINATION

610 Fifth Avenue

Even before the U.S. entered World War II, British Security Coordination (BSC) engaged the Axis powers in spy-vs.-spy operations in New York City. One included a woman—known only as "Madame Cadet"—who was the secretary to the financial attaché in the Vichy French consulate at ***610 Fifth Avenue.*** 21 After a BSC agent seduced her, she provided confidential telegrams confirming the existence of Nazi sympathizers in Quebec, Canada. When "Mme. Cadet" was transferred to Washington, D.C., she was handed off to another BSC agent, to whom she provided blank passports and official stamps that supported other espionage operations.

Another successful BSC operation involved an explosive propaganda campaign waged against Kurt Heinrich Rieth, a Nazi undercover agent who had entered the U.S. in 1941. Operating in the shadows of international trade, Rieth was a skilled diplomat from a wealthy German family (his father represented Standard Oil in Hamburg). After setting himself up in a $600-a-night luxury suite at the Waldorf-Astoria, he began working his business contacts with Standard Oil of New Jersey and other companies. Based on their intelligence about Rieth's activities, BSC leaked details to the press. Within days, The *New York Herald-Tribune* blared a headline: NAZI AGENT HERE ON SECRET MISSION SEEKS OIL HOLDINGS. Standard Oil denied ever hearing of Mr. Rieth, who locked himself in his hotel suite and refused to answer questions other than to say he was in New York on personal business. Five days after the headlines first appeared, he was deported.

AFTER A BSC AGENT SEDUCED HER, SHE PROVIDED CONFIDENTIAL TELEGRAMS CONFIRMING THE EXISTENCE OF NAZI SYMPATHIZERS IN QUEBEC, CANADA.

During the early days of World War II, the Vichy French operated out of this Rockefeller Center building—a short walk down the street from British intelligence headquarters.

MICHAEL KORS
610
MICHAEL KORS

LM22

UNDERCOVER RECRUITING

CLAYTON KNIGHT COMMITTEE

Knight Studio, 291 Fifth Avenue

At the start of World War II in 1939, Clayton Knight was an artist living in Greenwich Village with a studio at ***291 Fifth Avenue***. 22 His days as a World War I pilot were long behind him when he was contacted unexpectedly by Canadian flying ace Billy Bishop. Bishop described England as woefully unprepared for an air war and in desperate need of pilots. The two recruited E. Homer Smith, heir to a Canadian oil fortune, to launch the Clayton Knight Committee. Run from a luxury suite at the ***Waldorf-Astoria, 301 Park Avenue,*** 6 they recruited American pilots for training in Canada and onward deployment to Europe. The committee opened branches in Atlanta, Los Angeles, Chicago, Cleveland, and other major cities. Discreet posters and word of mouth attracted applicants, and for eighteen months, the committee supplied a steady stream of pilots to Canada.

The committee faced continuing legal problems because America was officially neutral and legal barriers prohibited Americans fighting in the armed services of foreign nations. Officially, the Clayton Knight Committee recruited for a private enterprise called Dominion Aeronautical Association, not the Canadian military. However, because of DAA's close ties to the Royal Canadian Air Force, the FBI and the State Department launched investigations. Knight staunchly maintained the committee was simply interviewing, providing physicals, giving flight tests, and then recommending applicants to a Canadian company. New York Mayor Fiorello LaGuardia turned a blind eye to the operation, as did President Roosevelt.

When America entered World War II, the committee was no longer needed and Knight turned his artistic attention to painting recruiting posters for the United States Army Air Force (USAAF) and patriotic illustrations of air combat for magazines. At the end of the war, Knight was awarded the Order of the British Empire.

One of New York City's premier luxury hotels, the Waldorf-Astoria has hosted heads of state, movie stars, and spies. Its art deco design remains as breathtaking today as when it opened its doors in the 1930s.

THE MILLIONAIRE SPY

VINCENT ASTOR

The Astor Home, 120 East End Avenue

The scion of one of New York's most prominent families, Vincent Astor inherited an estimated $200 million when his father, John Jacob Astor IV, died in the *Titanic* disaster in 1912. Vincent, the childhood friend of President Franklin Roosevelt, built his own apartment house residence at ***120 East End Avenue,*** 23 became an enthusiastic amateur spy, and was a founding member of "the Room," in a townhouse at ***34 East 62nd Street***. 24 The Room served as a private meeting place for tycoons, media giants, and other like-minded gentlemen such as Nelson Doubleday, Kermit Roosevelt, and David K. Bruce–all of whom would later become key players in the OSS. At the start of World War II, the name of the organization changed to the Club. In 2006, an unexplained explosion destroyed the townhouse.

Dispatched by President Roosevelt on a secret mission in 1938, Astor sailed his 263-foot oceangoing yacht, *Nourmahal*, with a 42-member crew and sophisticated radio equipment, to the Marshall Islands to report on Japanese activity in the region. He also investigated the cause of a calamitous fire aboard the SS *Normandie*, which resulted in its destruction and capsizing while undergoing conversion to a troop ship in 1942. Additionally, as a director of Western Union Cable Company, Astor was able to read international cables and piece together useful intelligence.

THE ROOM SERVED AS A PRIVATE MEETING PLACE FOR TYCOONS, MEDIA GIANTS, AND OTHER LIKE-MINDED GENTLEMEN

WORLD
WAR II

Once World War II erupted in Europe in 1939, New York again became a clandestine battlefield for England, Japan, and Germany. From midtown's luxury hotels and restaurants to the quiet, tree-lined streets of the outer boroughs, spies gathered intelligence, recruited agents, and sought to influence American opinion. The unprecedented wartime intelligence cooperation between the BSC and the OSS would serve as the foundation for America's own foreign intelligence organization—the CIA. After the war, as the United Nations rose on New York's East River as a symbol of the shared international vision for lasting peace, it also became a hotbed of international intelligence activities.

MT1

SPY HEADQUARTERS AT ROCK CENTER

BRITISH SECURITY COORDINATION

630 Fifth Avenue, International Building of Rockefeller Center

Beginning before World War II, Room 3603 (or 3553) at the *International Building of Rockefeller Center at 630 Fifth Avenue* 1 housed the BSC, which operated under nominal cover as the British Passport Control Office. The New York office of the OSS was later located conveniently nearby in Room 3663. Guarded by a 45-foot-high art deco statue of Atlas supporting a globe at its Fifth Avenue entrance, both American and British spymasters, William Donovan and William Stephenson, coordinated operations from the prestigious midtown address throughout the war.

World War II British intelligence operations were headquartered in Rockefeller Center. Located on bustling Fifth Avenue and featuring multiple entrances and exits, spies could slip in and out of the building unnoticed.

MT7

DEATH OF A JAYWALKING SPY

THE LUDWIG SPY RING

Hotel Taft (now the Michelangelo), 152 West 51st Street

Rain fell the evening of March 18, 1941, when a middle-aged, well-dressed man, wearing horn-rimmed spectacles and carrying a brown briefcase, stepped into traffic near the corner of *45th Street and Seventh Avenue*, 2 was struck by a cab, and propelled into the path of another car. An ambulance rushed him to St. Vincent's Hospital in Greenwich Village (closed in 2010), where he died the next day without recovering consciousness. The man was identified as Don Julio Lopez Lido, a Spanish citizen with a home address in Shanghai and guest of the *Hotel Taft (now the Michelangelo) at 152 West 51st Street.* 7 The Spanish consulate claimed the body and paid for the funeral.

The incident seemed like just another big-city tragedy, except for some troublesome details. First, Lopez Lido's companion at the scene of the accident had suspiciously grabbed the mortally injured man's briefcase and fled, vanishing into the gathering Times Square crowd. Second, a notebook found on the victim, written in German, contained names and assignments of U.S. soldiers. Third, his clothing bore no identifying labels. More suspicions mounted after a search of his hotel room uncovered a *Fortune* magazine article detailing the history of aviation, a story in *Harper's* magazine about "ferry pilots" flying bombers to Britain, and the book *Winged Warfare* by Major General H. H. Arnold and Colonel Ira C. Eaker.

THE INCIDENT SEEMED LIKE JUST ANOTHER BIG CITY TRAGEDY, EXCEPT FOR SOME TROUBLESOME DETAILS.

Even more clues emerged after British censors in a Bermuda mail-opening operation intercepted a letter from New York found to contain secret writing informing Lopez Lido's handlers that an American car had mysteriously run over and killed "PHIL." BSC notified the FBI that PHIL was actually Captain Ulrich von der Osten of the German *Abwehr* (military intelligence), who had entered the U.S. one month earlier from Japan.

Piecing together the clues, the FBI identified the victim's companion as an American citizen, Kurt Frederick Ludwig, who moved to Germany at an early age, then returned to the U.S. and was living in a boarding house on *Fresh Pond Road* in the Ridgewood section of Queens. He was also working as an agent for the German consulate.

By keeping Ludwig under surveillance, the FBI eventually identified six other members of the spy ring, including 18-year-old Lucy Boehmler of *62-02 60th Street, Maspeth, Queens.* The teenager functioned as Ludwig's $25-a-week secretary. Writing with a toothpick dipped in secret ink, Boehmler composed meticulous records regarding Army airfields, camps, and factories engaged in manufacturing wartime matériel. The final piece of the puzzle fell into place when Ludwig tried to bribe a police officer to send a telegram to the last member of the ring, Paul Borchardt. In all, eight other members of the spy ring, including a Long Island housewife and active military personnel, were eventually rounded up in the summer of 1941. Ludwig received a 20-year prison sentence. Boehmler, who testified for the prosecution, was sentenced to five years. All were released after the war.

TWO LADIES AND THE SPY

DUSAN "DUSKO" POPOV'S PENTHOUSE

530 Park Avenue

Nothing was low profile about World War II double agent Dusko Popov. He lived in this luxury Park Avenue building and dated beautiful women, including French film star Simone Simon. His extravagant lifestyle earned the admiration of James Bond creator Ian Fleming, and the ire of FBI chief J. Edgar Hoover.

Dusan Popov, a Yugoslavian businessman, was first recruited by the German *Abwehr* before volunteering to become a double agent for British intelligence. Given the code name TRICYCLE for his proclivity for entertaining two women at once, Popov became a valuable agent as well as a source of information on German tradecraft, like the microdot system used for covert communications. He was also adept at relaying disinformation to Berlin.

In addition to his fondness for beautiful women, Popov possessed an appetite for expensive living. Arriving in New York in 1941 on a secret mission for German military intelligence, he checked into a suite at the ***Waldorf-Astoria, 301 Park Avenue,*** 6 before taking up residence in a penthouse of a new luxury building just up the street at *530 Park Avenue.* 3 Never fully trusted by J. Edgar Hoover's FBI because of his flamboyant lifestyle, Popov complained to his British handlers, "Why, if I bend over to smell a bowl of flowers, I scratch my nose on a [FBI] microphone."

Neither Popov nor Hoover relented in their mutual disdain. The FBI chief finally threatened to have the spy arrested after learning he had taken a woman from New York to Florida for "immoral purposes"—illegal at the time under the Mann Act. Popov left the U.S. soon afterward, but played a key role in the 1944 Operation Fortitude deception campaign during the buildup to the Normandy landings in France.

In Popov, the FBI missed an intelligence opportunity by failing to recognize the significance of a microdot he was carrying that contained "tasking requirements" for the agent during his U.S. mission. These involved detailed questions, apparently requested by Germany's ally Japan, about U.S. defenses at Pearl Harbor. Decades later, Popov alleged that he informed the FBI on August 12, 1941, of the impending attack. Hoover forwarded the information to the Navy Department, but no action was taken.

> **"TO SURVIVE THE MULTIPLE HAZARDS OF ESPIONAGE IT IS BETTER NOT TO BE TOO SERIOUS".**
>
> **– Dusko Popov, legendary double agent during World War II**

SAVED BY THE MAFIA?

"LUCKY" LUCIANO'S GRAVE

St. John's Cemetery, Queens

More than a hundred merchant ships were sunk by German U-Boats off the Atlantic coast after America's entry into World War II. With such action close to shore, the U.S. feared that sabotage of American shipping ports could be the next move by the Axis powers. In response, the Office of Naval Intelligence contacted the Mafia for assistance in a secret activity code named OPERATION UNDERWORLD.

Mob kingpin Charles "Lucky" Luciano was easy to find at the Clinton Correctional Facility in upstate Dannemora, New York, where he was serving a 30–50 year sentence. Offered future clemency for cooperation, Luciano agreed to rally the underworld, including the Fulton Fish Market's Joseph Lanza, to safeguard the piers from sabotage and keep the fishing fleet free of rogue elements who might be tempted to sell fuel to surfacing U-Boats. In 1942, "Lucky" was transferred to better quarters at Great Meadows Correctional Facility in Comstock, N.Y. After the war, government authorities were apparently satisfied with the bargain. On January 3, 1946, the mobster was driven under guard to Pier 7 of the sprawling Bush Terminals (now Industry City) in Brooklyn, given a rousing bon voyage party, and put on the *Laura Paine,* which set sail for Italy. When Luciano died in 1962, his body was returned for burial at ***St. John's Cemetery in Queens.*** 4

HITLER'S FAILED SABOTEURS

OPERATION PASTORIUS

Governor Clinton (now Affinia Manhattan) Hotel, 371 Seventh Avenue at 31st Street

Once called the Governor Clinton, this landmark hotel was built in 1929 near Pennsylvania Station. Home to famous personalities, including inventor Nicola Tesla, it also briefly hosted two of Hitler's spies, George John Dasch and Ernest Peter Burger, during Operation Pastorius.

By mid-1942, American factories were working at full capacity building the warships, planes, and tanks needed to defeat the Axis powers. To disrupt military production, Hitler and his generals planned to bring the war to American soil by sending *Abwehr* agents to sabotage U.S. war production. Designated Operation Pastorius, the plan was named for the first German settlement in America, near Philadelphia.

Just after midnight on June 13, 1942, four men infiltrated onto a *Long Island beach near Amagansett* from U-Boat 584. They dragged ashore explosives, primers and incendiary devices, and more than $175,000 in cash to support two years of sabotage. Four days later, in the second phase of Operation Pastorius, U-Boat 202 delivered a similarly equipped group to Ponte Vedra Beach near Jacksonville, Florida.

The New York saboteurs were led by George John Dasch and included Ernest Peter Burger, Heinrich Harm Heinck, and Richard Quirin. All members of the New York and Florida teams were German nationals who had spent significant time in the U.S. before the war.

Almost immediately, the New York team ran into trouble. A Coast Guardsman on watch, armed with a flare gun, encountered the four would-be saboteurs as they were burying their equipment and changing from military uniforms into civilian clothing. Clumsily shoving about $260 cash into the surprised sentry's hands, they escaped up the beach, but the guardsman promptly reported the encounter to his superiors. Knowing they were compromised, the four caught the Long Island Railroad to Manhattan and broke into two groups. Dasch and Burger checked into the ***Governor Clinton, now Affinia Manhattan, 371 Seventh Avenue at 31st Street,*** 5 while Heinck and Quirin rented rooms at the ***Hotel Martinique, now the Radisson-Martinique, 49 West 32nd Street,*** 6 just off Broadway . The following night they rejoined for dinner and hit the town, going to clubs along Swing Street (West 52nd Street).

The Hotel Martinique's French Renaissance architecture might have appealed to German spies Heinrich Harm Heinck and Richard Quirin.

The next day, Dasch lost his nerve and called the New York FBI. The agent who answered the phone hung up on him, thinking it a prank call. Undeterred, Dasch took a train to Washington and surrendered to the FBI, revealing details of the plan along with descriptions of his fellow saboteurs.

Dasch's three companions were picked up in New York City on June 20. Two members of the Florida team were arrested on June 23, also in New York. The other two members of the Florida team were rounded up in Chicago on June 27.

From beginning to end, Operation Pastorius lasted less than two weeks. The eight were tried before a military commission, found guilty, and sentenced to death. Attorney General Francis Biddle and J. Edgar Hoover appealed to President Roosevelt to commute the sentences of Dasch and Burger. Dasch's sentence was reduced to thirty years in prison and Burger received life. The remaining six were executed at the District of Columbia jail on August 8, 1942. Three years after the war ended, President Truman granted executive clemency to Dasch and Burger on condition of deportation. Both were eventually freed in the American zone of Germany. Burger died in 1975 and Dasch in 1992.

"A BROKEN-DOWN BOARDING HOUSE" FOR SPIES

ST. REGIS HOTEL

2 East 55th Street

American and British spymasters met at this 1904-built hotel to plot strategies for World War II intelligence operations. Afterward, Ian Fleming used the hotel as a setting for James Bond's adventures.

The ***St. Regis, 2 East 55th Street,*** 7 catered to intelligence officers during World War II. General William "Wild Bill" Donovan was a frequent guest as he assembled America's first centralized intelligence service, the Office of the Coordinator of Information, which became the OSS in 1942. It was at the St. Regis that Donovan first met William Stephenson, the British spymaster who set up the BSC organization prior to the U.S. entry into World War II. Another British intelligence officer, Ian Fleming, liked the hotel so much he incorporated it into his James Bond novels *Diamonds Are Forever* and *Live and Let Die*. It is easy to imagine spies hatching plots in the hotel's iconic King Cole bar—said to be the birthplace of the Bloody Mary cocktail—with its Maxfield Parrish mural.

Built in 1904, the 18-story beaux-arts structure was owned by amateur spy and millionaire Vincent Astor, who referred to the luxury hotel as his "broken-down boarding house."

THE JAILBREAK THAT NEVER WAS

JACOB EPSTEIN

Residence, 958 Madison Avenue

In the early 1940s, the NKVD planned one of its boldest operations, code named GNOME, to break Trotsky assassin Jacques Mornard (true name Ramon Mercader) out of the *Palacio de Lecumberri* prison (known as The Black Palace of Lecumberri) in Mexico City. It would have been a daring escape, if it had happened. However, problems plagued the operation almost immediately, with scheduling conflicts, complicated logistics, and, finally, operational security. At the center of the plan was Jacob Epstein (code name HARRY), who lived at ***958 Madison Avenue.*** 8 Committed Communists, Epstein and his wife, Ruth Wilson Epstein (code name NONA), were to play integral roles in the Mexico City prison break.

One problem that arose early was in their covert communications with Moscow. In confusion or mishandled communications, Moscow sent an enciphered message asking the identity of "NONA." Incredibly, the New York *rezidentura* (NKVD station) responded, "NONA is Jacob Epstein's wife; that is to say, Ruth Wilson." Whether the NKVD placed too much trust in its code or it was just someone's first day on the job remains a mystery.

Delays and poor timing continued to hamper the plot until it eventually fizzled out as World War II began to heat up and Moscow itself was almost overrun by German troops following Operation BARBAROSSA in June of 1941. As for Mornard (Mercader), he served his full twenty years behind bars until released in 1960. Prison life, however, was not all bad—the NKVD sent Mornard money regularly and arranged for him to meet a Mexican B-list movie actress, whom he married and lived with periodically in a prison apartment.

Hailed as a hero in Russia following his release, Mornard, who had been identified as Ramon Mercader in 1950 by fingerprints, but never confirmed prior to his release, was presented with the honor hero of the Soviet Union. He divided his time between the Soviet Union and Cuba until his death in 1978.

LITTLE SHOP OF ESPIONAGE

UM9 VELVALEE DICKINSON'S DOLL SHOP

718 Madison Avenue

As Velvalee Dickinson's doll shop began to fail, she and her husband turned to spying for the Japanese. Today, the site is home to Beretta New York.

Velvalee Dickinson arrived in New York during the Great Depression, after her husband's San Francisco produce brokerage business failed. First taking a job in the doll department at Bloomingdale's, she subsequently opened her own doll shop at *680 Madison Avenue*, then moved up the street to *714 Madison,* and eventually settled in at ***718 Madison*** 9 in 1941. By the time Japan bombed Pearl Harbor in December 1941, the doll shop was failing, yet, inexplicably, the couple always seemed to have plenty of money for trips to the West Coast.

Then, in 1943, some American residents unexpectedly began receiving strange "return to sender" mail addressed to an Inez Lopez de Malinali in Buenos Aires, Argentina. The letters mysteriously bore U.S. return addresses of people with no knowledge of the correspondence. The contents, detailing doll sales, aroused suspicion, and a few were turned over to the FBI. From analysis of the letters, the FBI identified de Malinali as a Japanese intelligence contact in Buenos Aires and traced the letters back to Dickinson.

Something was hidden in the letters, but what? Breaking the "doll code" fell to Elizebeth Friedman, a veteran cryptographer, who discovered that each doll mentioned in the letters was a code for a specific type of American warship. Dickinson's intelligence had been gleaned from trips to the West Coast, where she observed shipyards and struck up conversations with employees.

With this discovery, authorities apprehended a kicking and screaming Dickinson in January 1944 at her bank, where a large amount of money was discovered in her safety deposit box. Dickinson was indicted for espionage, but a plea bargain reduced the charges to violating censorship laws. Sentenced to ten years in prison, she was paroled in 1951, vanished from sight in 1954, and is reported to have died in 1980.

THE SINGING SPY

MARLENE DIETRICH'S APARTMENT

993 Park Avenue at 83rd Street

When in New York City, Marlene Dietrich called 993 Park Avenue home. A naturalized U.S. citizen, the movie star worked tirelessly against the Nazis during the war years.

Movie star Marlene Dietrich resided at ***993 Park Avenue at 83rd Street*** 10 after becoming an American citizen in 1939. A tireless opponent to Nazism, the German immigrant celebrity sold war bonds, entertained troops, and worked for the OSS Morale Operations Branch. Dietrich, along with entertainers such as Bing Crosby and Dinah Shore, recorded songs aimed at lowering enemy morale and countering German propaganda. Dietrich's version of *Lili Marlene* for *Soldatensender (Soldiers Radio)* proved particularly powerful as a propaganda tool, inciting German soldiers to write letters of protest when it was banned by Nazi authorities. When Dietrich received the Presidential Medal of Freedom for her wartime support to OSS in 1945, she described the recognition as "the proudest accomplishment of her life." She died at age 90 on May 6, 1992.

DIETRICH, ALONG WITH ENTERTAINERS SUCH AS BING CROSBY AND DINAH SHORE, RECORDED SONGS AIMED AT LOWERING ENEMY MORALE AND COUNTERING GERMAN PROPAGANDA.

NOT TOO TALL TO SPY

JULIA CHILD'S APARTMENT

400 East 59th Street

Before becoming Julia Child the "famous chef," her name was Julia McWilliams, OSS officer from Pasadena. Her height of over six feet made Julia too tall for the Army or Navy, so she went to work for the Office of Strategic Services, first as a typist and then advancing to researcher for OSS director William "Wild Bill" Donovan. From that position, Child was posted in Sri Lanka and China. Her subsequent culinary fame has made her one of the OSS's legendary officers.

Like many college graduate women of her generation, Julia McWilliams began as a copywriter in New York, living in an apartment close enough to the East River to hear the waves against the pilings.

After graduating from Smith College in 1934, Child moved to her first New York apartment at ***400 East 59th Street*** 11 and began her professional career as an advertising copywriter for the now defunct W. J. Sloane home furnishings store at *575 Fifth Avenue*.

MAJOR LEAGUE SPY

MOE BERG BIRTHPLACE

East 121st Street

Born in a cold-water tenement on ***East 121st Street*** 12 in 1902, Morris "Moe" Berg studied at Princeton, then Columbia Law, and, briefly, the Sorbonne. After signing a professional baseball contract in 1923 at age 21, Berg played primarily as a catcher for a series of minor and major league teams, including the Brooklyn Robins (later called the Dodgers), Toledo Mud Hens, Chicago White Sox, Cleveland Indians, and Washington Senators. Casey Stengel once described Berg as "the strangest man ever to play baseball." Berg was certainly different from the other players; he spoke at least eight languages and read a half dozen newspapers a day, while compiling a journeyman's .243 lifetime batting average.

Just when Berg began spying is uncertain. Possibly it was in 1934, while playing an exhibition series in Japan. Sitting out a game, feigning illness, he donned traditional Japanese clothing and went onto a hospital roof to film the Tokyo skyline with a Bell and Howell 16mm camera, ostensibly for Movietone News. Once World War II began, Berg joined the OSS and worked behind enemy lines in Yugoslavia and then Nazi-occupied Norway.

However, perhaps Berg's most famous OSS assignment was Project AZUSA. The mission was to assess the state of the Nazi nuclear weapon program by attending a lecture by German physicist Werner Heisenberg in Switzerland in late 1944. If Berg, code name REMUS, judged the program close to producing a nuclear device, he was to shoot Heisenberg on the spot. The gun stayed in his pocket.

After the war, Berg undertook one final clandestine mission for the CIA. Between 1952–54, he was assigned to gather information about Soviet "atomic science." Eventually, the former ballplayer and spy drifted into public obscurity while maintaining a lifelong love for America's pastime. As he lay near death on May 29, 1972, the catcher-spy's last reported words were, "How are the Mets doing today?" They beat the Cardinals 7 to 6.

Morris "Moe" Berg, "the strangest man ever to play baseball."

THE TALKATIVE GANGSTER

OSS "TRUTH" DRUG

Belmont Plaza Hotel, 541 Lexington Avenue

Hopes were high in 1943 among OSS scientists that *tetrahydrocannabinol acetate*, a derivative of the cannabis plant, could elicit truth from an unsuspecting subject. To test the potential of this "truth serum," an OSS officer and former NYPD detective invited gangster August "Little Augie" Del Gaizo, whom he knew from his previous years in law enforcement, to a room at the ***Belmont Plaza Hotel, 541 Lexington Avenue,*** 13 now the W New York Hotel. The drug was administered to the unwitting Del Gaizo in a cigarette and appeared to have positive results when the gangster began describing some of his illegal activities. However, subsequent testing demonstrated the drug was unreliable and ineffective. Ten years later, under a top-secret program, MKULTRA, the CIA again tested the effects of drugs, including LSD, on human behavior with similar inconclusive results.

The Belmont Plaza Hotel, now the chic W Hotel New York, is reputed to have been the test site for an OSS truth serum.

COLD-FOOTED SABOTEURS

CAUGHT IN NEW YORK

Kenmore Hotel at 145 East 23rd Street

A German U-Boat quietly put two *Abwehr* spies ashore in Maine in November of 1944. Erich Gimpel, a German national with a background in radio work, and William Colepaugh, an American M.I.T. dropout, worked their way undetected from the shoreline, through Boston to New York, and checked into the ***Kenmore Hotel at 145 East 23rd Street.*** 14 Their mission was to collect intelligence and transmit it back to Germany by ciphered radio messages.

They spent the next few weeks subletting an apartment at ***39 Beekman Place***, 15 buying and modifying a shortwave radio, and living well on the German government's $60,000 in cash and stash of diamonds. They bought new clothes at stores near Rockefeller Center; watched *National Velvet* at Radio City Music Hall; and frequented New York City's then-classic nightspots like the *Copacabana, 10 East 60th Street; El Morocco, 154 East 54th Street;* and *The Stork Club, 3 East 53rd Street*. The money was quickly spent, and, just as quickly, Colepaugh decided he wasn't cut out for espionage. After confessing the nature of the mission to a friend from Queens, he told the story to the FBI. His partner, Gimpel, was soon arrested while buying a newspaper at the ***7th Avenue and 42nd Street*** 16 subway newsstand.

The mission, code named MAGPIE, lasted a little longer than a month. Tried on Governors Island before a military court, both were found guilty and sentenced to death. Fortunately for the pair, the war ended two months after their conviction, and President Truman reduced the sentences to life. Gimpel served ten years in Alcatraz before being paroled and returned to Germany. After Colepaugh was paroled in 1960, he married and settled in Pennsylvania.

NIGHTLIFE FOR SPIES

THE '21' CLUB

21 West 52nd Street

Originally called *Jack and Charlie's Place*, the townhouse at ***21 West 52nd Street***, 17 was a speakeasy before it became the internationally recognized *'21' Club.* Still operating at the same address today, the upscale eatery and bar was already legendary during World War II and attracted a diverse cross-section of patrons, including General "Wild Bill" Donovan of the OSS, FBI Director J. Edgar Hoover, and even

Ian Fleming and his fictional alter ego, James Bond, were both devotees of the '21' Club's famed wine cellar and menu.

The ultimate behind-the-scenes operator, Ernest Cuneo earned the trust of columnist Walter Winchell and President Franklin Roosevelt. As a liaison between British spies and American officials, Cuneo also became friends with Ian Fleming and Roald Dahl.

visiting German saboteurs. Ian Fleming, who frequented New York as a British intelligence officer, liked '21' so much he later incorporated it into his James Bond novels. In *Diamonds Are Forever*, Bond dines at '21' with the beautiful diamond-smuggling Bond Girl Tiffany Case.

One of Fleming's American contacts and a fellow '21' enthusiast was Ernest Cuneo. A New York insider, Cuneo worked as liaison between British intelligence, OSS, and President Roosevelt. Following the war, Cuneo married a British intelligence secretary and moved into a former Rockefeller-owned townhouse at ***9 East 62nd Street.*** 18 Cuneo maintained his friendship with Fleming and the pair often conducted "nightlife research" expeditions in New York, Las Vegas, and Chicago. Fleming's *Live and Let Die* is dedicated "To Ernest Cuneo, Muse."

FROM FASCIST TO COMMUNIST TO FBI SOURCE

LM20 ELIZABETH BENTLEY'S APARTMENT

58 Barrow Street

Elizabeth Bentley graduated from Vassar in 1930 and entered graduate school at *Columbia University*. During a fellowship in Italy, she flirted with fascism, but after returning to the U.S., swung to Communism. She soon came to the attention of Yakov Reizen, a Soviet intelligence officer in New York using the false identity of Jacob Golos, code name SOUND. Bentley first caught Golos's interest when she volunteered to spy on her Italian fascist friends. She later became his protégé and lover. Golos, then one of the Soviet Union's senior intelligence officers in the U.S., was subsequently involved in plans to assassinate Leon Trotsky. In 1938 Golos gave Bentley the code name UMNITSA (CLEVER GIRL) and put her to work as his courier and something of a spy "Girl Friday."

In 1940, Golos's company, World Tourists Inc., at *60 Fifth Avenue* and later at ***175 Fifth Avenue,*** 19 was exposed as an unregistered foreign

Soviet spy Elizabeth Bentley called this discreet West Village apartment home during some of her espionage career.

agent. Golos avoided arrest, but his cover was blown. With the spy network still intact, he set up another front company, *United States Service and Shipping at 212 Fifth Avenue,* with Bentley as vice president. Bentley lived in an apartment at ***58 Barrow Street***, 20 next to the former speakeasy Chumley's, with its multiple exits and secret passages.

Then, in 1943, Golos died of a heart attack in Bentley's apartment. Distraught and paranoid, she moved into the ***Hotel St. George at 100 Henry Street*** 21 in Brooklyn. Living in fear of both the FBI and her Soviet handlers, she began drinking heavily and acting increasingly erratic. She had good reason to be fearful; her Soviet handler in New York wanted her killed, but Moscow refused. By 1945, she had had enough and walked into the FBI field office in New York to tell her story. Bentley's confession exposed more than 100 Communists, including some thirty Soviet agents employed by the U.S. government. Bentley spent years testifying publicly about the dangers of Soviet espionage.

FROM SPY TO HOLLYWOOD

ROBERT RYAN'S APARTMENT

1 West 72nd Street, "The Dakota"

A graduate of Dartmouth College, actor Robert Ryan appeared in nearly 100 films, including *The Set-Up* (1949) and *The Wild Bunch* (1969), almost always playing tough-guy roles of a gangster, a gunslinger, or a boxer. The legendary star was indeed a tough Marine who reportedly worked closely with the OSS in Yugoslavia during World War II to assist partisan fighters. After the war, Ryan launched his movie career and became a champion of civil rights and liberal political causes. When he died in 1973, Ryan's apartment in New York's first luxury apartment house, The Dakota, at ***1 West 72nd Street,*** 22 was sold to John Lennon and Yoko Ono.

The Dakota acquired its name because some city dwellers thought its location was as remote as the Dakota Territory.

SEDUCING "THE SPY WHO SEDUCED AMERICA"

VALENTIN GUBITCHEV AND JUDITH COPLON

64 West 180th Street

For a brief time in 1949 and 1950, the American public couldn't get enough of Judith Coplon. Her multiple dramatic trials for espionage were the 1950s versions of a reality television show. The first American to be tried and convicted of spying for the Soviet Union after World War II, she was also the only Soviet agent identified from the highly secretive VENONA decryptions alone. Smart and ambitious, the petite girl from East Flatbush, Brooklyn, won a citizenship award at James Madison High School, *3787 Bedford Avenue, Brooklyn*, graduated *cum laude* from Barnard College, and went to work for the Department of Justice. Through a college friend and Soviet talent spotter, Flora Don Wovschin, code name ZORA, Coplon was recognized as a potential asset, recruited by the married Valentin Gubitchev, and given the code name SIMA in 1944. Gubitchev, code name CARP, worked out of the United Nations Secretariat's Department of Conferences and General Services at ***1270 Sixth Avenue,*** 23 commuting from his apartment at ***64 West 180th Street.*** 24 His recruitment of Coplon was uncomplicated; the Russian intelligence officer took the young woman for romantic walks to Rockefeller Center during the Christmas season, rowboating in Central Park during the summer, and to cozy dinners in Greenwich Village bistros before eventually seducing her.

"She [Coplon] gives the impression of a very serious, modest, thoughtful young woman . . . There is no question about the sincerity of her desire to work for us," read a report on her to Moscow. For five years, Coplon allegedly spied, until she was identified in 1948 by VENONA, the secret U.S. project working to decrypt intercepted Soviet wartime communications from 1942 to 1945.

Coplon and Gubitchev were eventually arrested in 1949 on *Third Avenue between 15th and 16th Streets*, tried, and convicted. Gubitchev, in the U.S. with diplomatic status, was deported. Coplon's conviction was overturned. Retried, she was convicted a second time, and again the verdict was invalidated on legal procedures. Coplon eventually married one of her lawyers, Albert Socolov, and ran two now defunct Manhattan restaurants, the Beach House in TriBeCa and Alameda on the Upper West Side. She died at age 89 in 2011.

SPIES TO THE END

MORRIS AND LEONTINA COHEN

Residence at 178 East 71st Street

U.S.-born Morris and Leontina Cohen were committed Communists who served as couriers in the Soviet penetration of America's atomic weapon development program. Morris used the code names LOUIS and VOLUNTEER, while his wife, Leontina, was LESLIE. Playing a supporting role in the Julius and Ethel Rosenberg operation, the pair also crossed paths in New York with Soviet spymaster Rudolph Abel. When Abel was arrested, the Cohens' passports were found in his bank safe-deposit box.

Between 1948 and 1950, the Cohens lived at ***178 East 71st Street*** 25 while Morris Cohen worked at a public school on *Lexington Avenue and East 96th Street.* Fearing discovery after the arrest of scientist and Soviet spy Klaus Fuchs in Great Britain in 1950, the couple told friends they were heading to Hollywood for screenwriting jobs and fled. Instead, they went to Moscow via Mexico, where Leontina received additional training in ciphers and as a radio operator. Next, they moved to England in 1954 on New Zealand passports as Helen and Peter Kroger. Settling in the quiet London suburb of East Ruislip, the pair ran a London antiquarian bookstore specializing in penology.

The Cohens' (Krogers') real work was supporting the London illegal *rezidentura* of Konon Trofimovich Molody, a Russian intelligence officer with the alias Gordon Lonsdale who ran the Portland spy ring. Their residence in East Ruislip was a covert communications center from which Molody's information was converted into microdots and concealed inside books shipped abroad. Molody was finally caught by MI5 using information from a Polish defector that eventually led to the Krogers. A search of the Krogers' residence revealed a secret radio transmitter buried under the house and accessed through a trapdoor beneath the refrigerator. The Cohens and Molody were convicted of spying in 1961. Leontina was sentenced to twenty years jail time while her husband was given twenty-five years. After serving eight years, the Cohen's were exchanged in a spy swap and relocated to Moscow where they died years later, Leontina in 1992 and Morris in 1995.

TOUGH SPOUSE OF AMERICA'S SPYMASTER

CLOVER AND ALLEN DULLES

Home at 239 East 61st Street

A townhouse at ***239 East 61st Street*** 26 was home to Allen Dulles, future director of the Central Intelligence Agency, when he worked as a lawyer in the Wall Street firm Sullivan & Cromwell and later with the OSS. During World War II, while Allen was in Switzerland with the OSS, his wife, Clover, lived in the Upper East Side townhouse and commuted by subway to her job in Brooklyn as a defense plant supervisor. After Clover took a firm stand against what she viewed as racial discrimination in the plant, one factory worker said to her, "You're probably the toughest son-of-a-bitch in the place!"

Dulles became the first and longest serving civilian director of the CIA, holding the position from 1953 to 1961. Later, he served as a member of the Warren Commission investigating President Kennedy's assassination. Dulles is considered one of the creators of the modern U.S. intelligence community.

THE SPY AND THE MOVIE STAR

ROALD DAHL

Residence, 44 West 77th Street

Roald Dahl, beloved children's book author of *Charlie and the Chocolate Factory* and *James and the Giant Peach*, was also a spy during World War II. Attached to the BSC as a liaison officer to the Office of Strategic Services, the future author made frequent trips to New York. Following the war, Dahl devoted his time to writing and spent substantial time in New York. His first New York City address was *East 92nd Street, just off Fifth Avenue*. In July 1953, Dahl married Academy Award–winning movie star Patricia Neal at *Trinity Church (Broadway and Wall Street)*. The couple split their time between England and America living in a series of New York City apartments at ***44 West 77th Street*** 27 and ***26 East 81st Street.*** 28

Roald Dahl and actress Patricia Neal lived on the Upper East Side, across from the Frank E. Campbell Funeral Chapel.

One of Dahl's recollections of the early post-war years was a train ride he took with Ian Fleming, a fellow wartime British intelligence officer. When discussing their post-war plans, Fleming mentioned he was writing a novel about a fictional secret agent. Dahl, already an accomplished author, dismissed the idea that such a story would sell and suggested that Fleming "get a real job instead." Ignoring the advice, Fleming published *Casino Royale* in 1952, introducing James Bond, the world's most recognized spy.

New York was the frontline of Cold War intelligence operations. Some of the USSR's and America's greatest espionage successes and failures took place in the city. Not only was New York the hub of Rudolph Abel's "atomic spy" network, several of America's most significant Soviet recruitments occurred in the city. Primarily working from their respective UN missions, foreign intelligence officers used every neighborhood of every borough for recruitments, dead drops, brush passes, and clandestine meetings. These "cold warriors" worked quietly in the shadows, but when exposed or arrested by the FBI, their cases became front-page news.

THE SPY WHO SAVED THE YANKEES

OLD YANKEE STADIUM

1 East 161st Street, The Bronx

E. Michael Burke

Turning down a contract with the Philadelphia Eagles football team, E. Michael Burke opted to join the OSS during World War II. Infiltrated into Italy and then France, Burke worked with the Resistance in preparation for D-Day. Awarded the Navy Cross, the Silver Star, and the French *Medaille de la Resistance*, Burke returned home a hero. In 1946, he landed in Hollywood as a technical advisor to the 1946 film *Cloak and Dagger,* starring Gary Cooper and Lilli Palmer. The film was purportedly based on Burke's wartime exploits. Burke left Hollywood and in 1949 joined the CIA, where he spent his next five years.

However, among baseball fans, Burke is better known as the man who kept the Yankees in New York. In 1964, as a CBS executive, he was instrumental in the network's purchase of the team for $13.2 million. Later, in exchange for not moving the Yankees to New Jersey, Burke negotiated a deal with the city to rebuild the "House that Ruth Built" at *1 East 161st Street, The Bronx.* 1

A FUTURE PRESIDENT INVESTIGATES SPYING

GRAND HYATT HOTEL

109 East 42nd Street at Grand Central Terminal

Behind the Grand Hyatt's reflective glass lies the espionage history of the landmark Commodore Hotel.

The extensively refurbished **Grand Hyatt at** ***109 East 42nd Street at Grand Central Terminal*** 2 was originally named the Commodore Hotel after railroad tycoon Cornelius "Commodore" Vanderbilt. In room 1400, members of a special subcommittee of the Committee of Un-American Activities, including future President Richard Nixon, met in an explosive executive session on August 17, 1948. In a dramatic confrontation, U.S. State Department official Alger Hiss identified writer Whittaker Chambers as the man he knew as "George Crosley"–a member of a Soviet spy ring. Nixon used the hearings to bolster his anti-Communist political image. Questions of loyalty and charges of lying by supporters of both Hiss and Chambers continued throughout the Cold War.

THE KGB SLEPT HERE

A HOME FOR SOVIET SPIES

355 West 255th Street, The Bronx

Guarded by sentries, heavy steel gates, and state-of-the-art surveillance cameras, a compound on a hilltop in the Riverdale section of The Bronx is home to Russian diplomats accredited to the UN.

If you were a Soviet intelligence officer under diplomatic cover in New York, you most likely lived at an apartment in the *Riverdale section of the Bronx at 355 West 255th Street.* 3 Twenty stories of unadorned concrete at the center of a fenced compound on a hill provided living quarters and a social center for Soviet officials stationed in New York during the Cold War. Before the compound's construction, Soviet officials lived in hotels like the *Excelsior at 45 West 81st Street* 4 and the *Esplanade at 305 West End Avenue*, 5 now a senior residential facility. Both were targets of FBI eavesdropping operations under the code name MEGAHUT.

Cold War tensions made the Riverdale property a flash point in local politics. Since occupying the compound in the 1970s, the Soviets have battled neighbors, protesters, and the local zoning board along with assaults, including gunshots and at least one bomb attack. In 1982, Bronx Borough President Stanley Simon renamed the street Anatoly Shcharansky (sic) Square to show support for the jailed Russian dissident. The small ceremony and new street sign at *255th Street and Mosholu Avenue* set off a small diplomatic incident.

Higher-ranking officials had residences at the Soviet UN mission, at *136 East 67th Street,* 6 now the home of the permanent mission of the Russian Federation to the UN, while the most privileged were given allowances for their own apartments. New York was considered a plum assignment, and at times as many as 300 Soviet intelligence officers lived throughout the city under "diplomatic cover."

RADIOACTIVE SPIES

THE ROSENBERGS' RESIDENCE

10 Monroe Street, Apt. GE-11, Knickerbocker Village

The controversy surrounding the arrest and execution of "Atomic Spies" Julius and Ethel Rosenberg lasted for four decades.

One of America's most closely held secrets of the Cold War was VENONA, the code name for the breaking of encrypted Soviet secure communications intercepted between 1942 and 1945. The effort revealed a nationwide Soviet intelligence network intently focused on acquiring secrets of the atomic bomb.

The most widely recognized of the USSR's atomic spies were Julius Rosenberg, code name LIBERAL and ANTENNA, and his wife, Ethel, who lived at *10 Monroe Street, apartment GE-11 in the Knickerbocker Village* 7 housing project on the Lower East Side. A dedicated Communist, Julius Rosenberg was recruited by Soviet intelligence officer Jacob Golos, code name SOUND, in 1942. Julius recruited Ethel in 1944 and the couple served as couriers, cutouts, and recruiters. Next, the Rosenbergs recruited Ethel's brother, David Greenglass, code name CALIBER, who was a machinist on the Manhattan Project and living at *266 Stanton Street* 8 on the Lower East Side.

Known as the "Atomic Spies" when they were arrested in 1950, the Rosenbergs were found guilty of espionage in 1951 and executed in June of 1953 at the Sing Sing Correctional Facility, in Ossining, N.Y., thirty miles north of New York City. The arrest of the Rosenbergs and coconspirators prompted outcries of anti-Semitism against the U.S. legal system, and conspiracy theories thrived. Controversy continued for four decades until the declassification of the VENONA materials in 1995 provided conclusive evidence implicating the Rosenbergs and also revealing the particularly virulent anti-Semitism freely expressed by Soviet intelligence officers, who used the Russian word for "rats" as a code name for American Jews.

FINAL

DAILY NEWS

NEW YORK'S PICTURE NEWSPAPER

4¢

SPIES DIE IN CHAIR

The Rosenbergs were executed in 1953.

FILMS AND SPIES

MT9 ARTKINO PICTURES INC.

723 Seventh Avenue

Amid the bright lights of Times Square, film distributor Artkino brought Soviet films like *Ballad of Siberia* (1947) and *Cossacks of the Kuban* (1949) to American audiences.

For more than four decades beginning in the 1930s, Nicola Napoli, president of Artkino Pictures, ***723 Seventh Avenue,*** 9 was the primary distributor of Soviet films in the United States. Less well known was his role in passing information to the Communist Party U.S.A. (CPUSA), and Soviet intelligence during WWII.

Napoli became involved in supporting Soviet intelligence after he came to the attention of Jacob Golos, code name SOUND, a founding member of the CPUSA. Shortly before his death of a heart attack in 1943, Golos told his protégé and agent Elizabeth Bentley, code name CLEVER GIRL, that he was turning Napoli over to another Russian contact to continue their covert relationship. Napoli was later identified in a decrypted VENONA Soviet communication sent in December 1944 by the NKVD in New York to Moscow.

Also revealed as a spy in the VENONA decrypts was Theodore Alvin Hall, code name MLAD or MLAS, meaning "youth." The youngest physicist to work on the atomic bomb project at Los Alamos, Hall, along with college friend Saville Sax, made numerous attempts to "walk in" and offer his services as a spy. Approaching CPUSA head Earl Browder, the young men were rebuffed by his secretary, but the pair had better luck with Napoli, who handed Hall off to Soviet intelligence officer Sergi Kournakoff, code names CALVERYMAN and BEK, whose cover job was as a journalist at the *Daily Worker*. Hall would later provide a detailed description of the Fat Man plutonium bomb, as well as processes for purifying plutonium, to Soviet intelligence.

THE PHYSICS OF ESPIONAGE

KLAUS FUCHS

128 West 77th Street

British physicist and Soviet spy Klaus Fuchs held high security clearances when he worked on America's atomic bomb in the Manhattan Project.

Physicist Klaus Fuchs, code names REST, CHARLES, and BRAS, spied for the Soviets first in England, then in the U.S., and again in England. He lived for a time at ***Hotel Taft, now the Michelangelo, at Seventh Avenue and 50th Street,*** 7 then the *Barbizon-Plaza Hotel (now the Trump Parc East) at 106 Central Park South*. His last New York address was at ***128 West 77th Street.*** 10 Having already passed information about America's top secret nuclear program in Oak Ridge, Tennessee, to the Soviets, he was assigned to Los Alamos, New Mexico, and continued his spying.

It was not until after World War II, when Fuchs returned to Great Britain to work on that country's nuclear program, that he came under scrutiny by the FBI. The FBI shared its suspicions with its British counterparts. MI5 began questioning Fuchs in late 1949, and he confessed to espionage in early 1950. Since the Soviet Union was considered an ally during World War II, Fuchs could not be convicted of high treason, a capital offense. Found guilty of a lesser charge, he was sentenced to fourteen years in prison before being released in 1959. Fuchs immigrated to East Germany and became director of that country's Institute of Nuclear Physics, a post he held until retiring in 1979. He died in 1988.

SINCE THE SOVIET UNION WAS CONSIDERED AN ALLY DURING WORLD WAR II, FUCHS COULD NOT BE CONVICTED OF HIGH TREASON, A CAPITAL OFFENSE.

COLD WAR MASTER SPY

RUDOLPH IVANOVICH ABEL

Studio at 252 Fulton Street, Brooklyn

Rudolph Abel was the chief Russian illegal in the U.S. after the collapse of the wartime Soviet networks and the FBI's biggest counterintelligence success at the time of his arrest in 1957. Abel, whose given name was Vilyam Genrikhovich Fisher, operated under multiple alias names including Andrew Kyotis, Emil Goldfus, and Mark Collins. He spoke nearly flawless Polish and German to match his varied identities. However, it was the Soviet illegal's fluent English, spoken with a slight British accent and a touch of Brooklynese, that allowed him to blend into his Brooklyn neighborhood. From this location, Abel, code name MARK, who entered the U.S. in 1948, rebuilt the wartime VOLUNTEER espionage network that smuggled atomic secrets to the USSR. In 1950, he rented an apartment at *216 West 99th Street.*

Soviet spy Rudolph Abel called this apartment on West 99th Street home during his first months in New York City.

A talented painter, excellent photographer, accomplished linguist, and amateur musician, Abel was also a master at tradecraft. He constructed many of his own concealment devices, which included pieces of jewelry, hollowed-out pencils, and artist's tools. Other artists in the ***Ovington Building at 252 Fulton Street, Brooklyn,*** **12** where he maintained a studio, saw only a mild-mannered older man always willing to lend a hand. "I wish I had a couple like him in Moscow," CIA head Allen Dulles later commented.

Abel conducted operations throughout the city's boroughs, including *Fort Tyron Park* in Upper Manhattan where he located dead drop sites under lamp posts; the ***Symphony Theatre at Broadway and 95th Street;*** **13** ***Prospect Park, Brooklyn;*** **14** the cement wall between *165th and 167th Streets on Jerome Avenue, the Bronx;* ***Central Park's Bridle Path Bridge;*** **15** and under mailboxes between *74th and 79th Streets along Central Park West.*

The "master spy's" downfall was his undisciplined, hard-drinking assistant, Reino Häyhänen, code name VIC and known as Eugene Nicolai Maki, who defected to the West in Paris in 1957. Having once visited the site of Abel's studio, Häyhänen tipped off the FBI to the location. Agents then staked out the illegal's Brooklyn studio and apartment before spotting and trailing Abel to room 839 at the *Latham Hotel, 4 East 28th* Street, 16 where he was arrested on June 21, 1957.

Master Soviet spy Rudolph Abel was apprehended by the FBI at the Latham in 1957.

The arrest solved the mystery of a hollow nickel containing microfilm with ciphered information that a drunk Häyhänen mistakenly spent. The nickel eventually turned up in the hands of a young Brooklyn newspaper boy, James Bozart, in 1953, after collecting payments from customers at ***3403 Foster Avenue.*** 11 When Bozart accidentally dropped the nickel, it split apart—revealing the cavity and microfilm. Häyhänen's defection also provided the FBI with the key to decrypt the message.

WHEN BOZART ACCIDENTALLY DROPPED THE NICKEL, IT SPLIT APART—REVEALING THE CAVITY AND MICROFILM.

Abel was tried, convicted, and sentenced to 30 years in prison in the fall of 1957. Five years later, the illegal was swapped for downed American U-2 pilot Francis Gary Powers and honored as a hero when he returned to Moscow. Despite his status as a Soviet "spy hero," KGB colleagues knew that it was Abel's tradecraft error in taking Häyhänen to his studio in Brooklyn that violated the compartmentation of the network and led directly to Abel's detection and arrest.

GRU AND KGB COVER COMPANY

AMTORG TRADING COMPANY

49 West 37th Street

Founded by Armand Hammer with help from Vladimir Lenin, AMTORG was used by the Soviets as a commercial cover for espionage.

If you wanted to find a Soviet military intelligence officer in New York during the Cold War, the American Trading Organization (AMTORG) was a likely location. Set up by American businessman Armand Hammer in 1924 to represent Soviet trade in the U.S., the GRU packed the firm with intelligence officers under commercial cover. Its multiple New York addresses over the years included *165 Broadway, 261 Fifth Avenue, 238 West 28th Street,* ***49 West 37th Street,*** 17 and *210 Madison Avenue.* FBI Special Agent (and spy) Robert Hanssen first made contact with Soviet intelligence by walking into AMTORG's New York office in 1979 and volunteering. At the time, Hanssen and his family were living at *150 Webster Road in Scarsdale*, an affluent suburb in Westchester County. After Hanssen's wife caught him spying, he suspended his espionage activity until 1985, when he volunteered in Washington, D.C., this time to the KGB. Hanssen used a variety of alias and code names, including RAMON.

MAIL CENSORSHIP

LESSONS FROM THE BRITISH

Idlewild (now JFK) Airport

John F. Kennedy International Airport, known until 1963 as ***Idlewild Airport***, 18 was for several years home to a secret CIA mail-opening operation that began in 1952. Code named SRPOINTER and later HTLINGUAL, the operation examined an estimated 215,000 pieces of mail from and to Soviet Bloc countries over two decades.

The envelopes were collected within a restricted area of Federal Building No. 111, known as the Jamaica Airmail Facility, adjoining the airport. During the evening, a CIA team would photograph envelope exteriors with a Diebold camera, then select some for opening. The method of opening was to hold the envelope over a steaming teakettle to soften the sealant, and then slip a narrow stick under the flap and remove the letter. Technicians tested suspect letters and envelopes for secret writing, sought evidence of microdots, and evaluated Soviet censorship techniques. After the letters were tested and photographed, they were put back into their envelopes, resealed, and returned to the mails the following morning.

HTLINGUAL was, in essence, a continuation of an earlier joint British-FBI mail-opening program to detect and intercept covert communications of enemy spies. During World War II, the work was done at a British facility in the basement of Bermuda's Princess Hotel, today the Fairmont Hamilton Princess. The staff was composed primarily of women, because women seemed better suited to a job requiring a high level of fine motor skills. According to former British spy H. Montgomery Hyde, after management observed that women with "neat ankles" seemed to perform the job particularly well, the FBI assigned an elderly agent to inspect the ankles of applicants, perhaps making it the most unusual screening processes ever for a government job.

It was dull, grueling work carried out in a basement in a tropical paradise. The young women assigned at the facility composed a song called "The Virgin's Lament," with the refrain:

I'm just a girl at MI-5
And heading for a virgin's grave–
My legs it was wot got me in–
Still I wait for my bit of sin–

I'M JUST A GIRL AT MI5
AND HEADING FOR A VIRGIN'S GRAVE–
MY LEGS IT WAS WOT GOT ME IN–
STILL I WAIT FOR MY BIT OF SIN–

– Composed by female staff at British mail-opening operation

BROTHERS IN ESPIONAGE

MORRIS AND JACK CHILDS

9th floor, 11 Broadway

Russian-born brothers Morris and Jack Childs were active in the Communist party in the 1920s before drifting away to pursue careers and get on with their lives. However, by the early 1950s, the two brothers returned to the Communist fold and quickly rose through the ranks, even traveling to Moscow and neutral countries to meet with handlers and receive training. In the 1960s, with the CPUSA running a deficit, Morris Childs, code name MARAT, received more than a million dollars a year from the Soviets to keep the organization going. A courier would execute a brush pass with Childs delivering the cash—always at 3:05 p.m.—at a variety of locations, including the 10th floor of *10 Pine Street*, code name DINO; 19 the 9th floor of *11 Broadway*, code name FRED; 20 the 7th floor of *120 Wall Street*, code name POST; 20 and the 2nd floor of *81 New Street*, code name ROLAND. 21

Morris and Jack Childs used Manhattan office buildings, including 11 Broadway, for clandestine meetings.

Soviet operational security for these brief encounters was near perfect. Each building was chosen for its multiple entrances and exits. The two brothers were in every respect superb agents—disciplined, calm, and reliable. They received the Order of the Red Banner in 1975, when Morris traveled to Moscow to accept the tribute during a banquet in his honor presided over by Leonid Brezhnev, general secretary of the Central Committee of the Communist Party of the USSR. However, the Childs's Soviet contacts in New York and Moscow did not know the brothers were skimming as much as 5% of the money passed from the CPUSA. Even more damaging, the Childs had been working as double agents for the FBI under the code name SOLO since rejoining the Communist Party in the early 1950s. Not until the 1980s, after decades of walking the double agent tightrope, were Soviet suspicions aroused and the operation closed down by the FBI. For their service, President Ronald Reagan awarded Morris and Jack (posthumously) the Presidential Medal of Freedom.

MT22

DEATH OF A SCIENTIST

THE STATLER HOTEL

Now the Pennsylvania, 401 Seventh Avenue

A government scientist jumped to his death here after participating in a CIA-sponsored LSD drug experiment.

The Statler Hotel at *401 Seventh Avenue* 22 gained fame with Glenn Miller's 1940 big-band hit song "PEnnsylvania 6-5000," though a darker chapter in the hotel's history occurred on November 27, 1953. From a tenth-floor window of the hotel, now the *Hotel Pennsylvania,* Dr. Frank Olson, a participant in a CIA drug testing program, MKULTRA, jumped to his death. After a two-decade effort to keep the operation and circumstances of Olson's death secret, MKULTRA was exposed and investigated by Congressional committees in the mid-1970s.

LM23

DRUGS, BOOZE, AND RUSSIAN SAILORS

OPERATION MIDNIGHT CLIMAX

81 Bedford Street in Greenwich Village

An apartment at this address on a quiet tree-lined street in the West Village was used for drug tests on unwitting subjects as part of the CIA's MKULTRA program.

During the early years of the Cold War, as part of the CIA's MKULTRA program to understand the effect of a variety of drugs on human behavior, experiments were conducted on witting and unwitting persons in New York and San Francisco. The unwitting subjects, to whom "truth drugs" were administered at an apartment at *81 Bedford Street in Greenwich Village,* 23 included Russian sailors. Prostitutes were paid to lure the sailors to the apartment, where they were secretly observed and photographed after consuming alcoholic beverages laced with drugs. Similar experiments occurred in an apartment in the Telegraph Hill section of San Francisco. Despite the public reports of Congressional investigations in the 1970s and more recent declassification of all surviving MKULTRA documents related to it, the program remains the subject of lingering conspiracy theories about its purpose and participants.

THE PASSWORD IS ABRACADABRA

JOHN MULHOLLAND RESIDENCE

600 West 115th Street

John Mulholland, the most skilled magician of his generation and a virtuoso of close-up magic, began a six-year secret association with the CIA in 1953. Working from his office at ***130 West 42nd Street*** (24) and his home at ***600 West 115th Street,*** (25) Mulholland wrote two training manuals for the agency that described basic magic principles and practices, such as the use of concealments, misdirection, and clandestine signaling. Funded through the MKULTRA program, the top secret manuals adapted magician stagecraft to tradecraft. Although most of the CIA's MKULTRA materials were destroyed in 1973 by order of Director Richard Helms, the Mulholland manuals were somehow missed. These remained classified until 2003, fifty years after their writing. Although by today's standards of performance magic Mulholland's tricks are elementary, the manuals offer a rare glimpse into the breadth of Cold War efforts to equip CIA officers with unconventional spy tools. Most enduring is Mulholland's underlying understanding that, in the words of former Acting DCI, John McLaughlin, "espionage and magic are kindred spirits."

"ESPIONAGE AND MAGIC ARE KINDRED SPIRITS."

– Former Acting DCI, John McLaughlin

MAFIA ASSASSINS

UM26 PLAZA HOTEL

Fifth Avenue and Central Park South

On September 14, 1960, a former FBI agent turned private investigator, Robert Maheu, acting as a CIA go-between, met former bootlegger and gangster John "Johnny" Roselli at the Plaza Hotel on *Fifth Avenue and Central Park South.* 26 The purpose of the meeting was to explore the possibility of recruiting the Mafia to assassinate the Cuban dictator, Fidel Castro, his brother, Raul, and Che Guevara. Following the initial discussion, the CIA's "targeted killing" operation, code named ZRRIFLE, dragged on in various forms for three years before fizzling out in late 1963. When the plot became public in the mid-1970s, it became a catalyst for the 1976 presidential executive order prohibiting any U.S. government employee from planning or conducting an assassination operation.

UPPER EAST SIDE TRAITOR

MT28 ALDRICH AMES RESIDENCE

The Revere, 400 East 54th Street

Before he became one of the most damaging spies of the 20th century, Aldrich Ames worked for the CIA from an office in the Pan Am Building (now the Met Life Building) at *200 Park Avenue.* 27 At the time, he and his first wife, Nan, lived in a one-bedroom apartment in a high-rise at *The Revere, 400 East 54th Street.* 28 While in New York, Ames was involved in major CIA operations including handling Sergey Fedorenko, a nuclear arms expert assigned to the Soviet United Nations

Before becoming a spy for the Soviets, Aldrich Ames ran intelligence operations against Russian diplomats in New York. He lived a quiet life of a government employee in this modest Upper East Side apartment building.

delegation, and the defection of Soviet undersecretary of political affairs at the United Nations, Arkady Shevchenko. In October 1985, a few years after leaving New York, Ames turned traitor.

The KGB gave Ames the code name KOLOKOL or "the Bell." During his nine years as a mole inside the CIA, Ames exposed more than a dozen Western agents operating in the USSR—at least ten of whom were executed. Ames continued spying for Russia until his arrest in February 1994. At the time of his capture, his Moscow savings account totaled $4.6 million. Ames used the "extra income" to finance a lavish lifestyle of expensive cars, jewelry, and clothing for himself and his second wife. He was convicted of espionage on April 28, 1994, and sentenced to life without parole.

QUIET PLEASE, SPIES AT WORK

NEW YORK PUBLIC LIBRARY

42nd Street and Fifth Avenue

"LIFE IN NEW YORK CITY MADE ME DO IT. IT WAS EXPENSIVE, DIRTY, AND A LOT OF CRIME, A LOT OF PEOPLE, VERY CONGESTED."

– Earl Edwin Pitts

FBI Special Agent Earl Edwin Pitts was recruited by the KGB in the law section of the *New York Public Library, 42nd Street and Fifth Avenue,* 29 after offering his services as a spy in a letter to the nearby Soviet mission. Of his espionage, Pitts told one reporter, "Life in New York City made me do it. It was expensive, dirty, and a lot of crime, a lot of people, very congested." Pitts was making an annual salary of $38,000 when assigned to the FBI's New York office in 1987.

From 1987 to 1992, Pitts passed secrets to his Soviet handlers, receiving more than $224,000 in payments. He was eventually identified after his KGB handler, Alexsandr Karpov, defected to the U.S. During the sixteen-month period he was under investigation, Pitts's wife, also an FBI employee, reported her suspicions that her husband was a spy. Convicted on June 27, 1997, Pitts is serving a 27-year prison sentence in a federal facility in Kentucky.

MIDNIGHT RECRUITMENT

GRANT'S TOMB

West 122nd Street and Riverside Drive

The imposing monument at *West 122nd Street and Riverside Drive* (30) was the 1962 site of the recruitment of Lt. General Dimitri Fedorovich Polyakov, one of America's most valuable Cold War spies. The Soviet GRU military intelligence officer, then working at the UN, is reported to have made initial contact with Americans at a cocktail reception and subsequently met clandestinely with an FBI agent at Grant's Tomb at midnight. Polyakov agreed to continue the secret contact and was given the FBI code name TOPHAT, after the Hanna-Barbera cartoon character.

One of America's most valuable spies was, fittingly, recruited during a midnight meeting at Grant's Tomb. As a Civil War general, Grant made extensive use of spies.

The case required close coordination between the FBI and CIA because Polyakov was handled by the FBI when in the U.S. and by the CIA when posted in foreign locations. The long-term agent, code named BOURBON and ROAM by the CIA, quietly retired in Russia in the early 1980s, only to be betrayed first by FBI Special Agent Robert Hanssen to the GRU and later by Aldrich Ames to the KGB. Polyakov was arrested in 1986 and executed in 1988.

AN AMERICAN IN THE CAMBRIDGE SPY RING

MICHAEL WHITNEY STRAIGHT

22 East 67th Street

Born into a privileged family, future spy Michael Whitney Straight spent his early childhood in a townhouse on *22 East 67th Street* (31) before moving to England with his parents. He attended Cambridge University in the 1930s, where he was recruited as an agent for the Soviets by Anthony Blunt and given the code name NIGEL.

From a luxurious townhouse on Manhattan's Upper East Side, Straight moved to England at a young age and was recruited as a Soviet agent.

Returning to the U.S. in 1937, Straight continued his espionage, sometimes meeting his Soviet handler, Iskhak Abdulovich Akhmerov, alias Michael Green, at the now-defunct upscale restaurant chain Longchamps. In the late 1930s, Straight volunteered at the State Department before leaving to edit his family's magazine, the *New Republic*. The prospect of a routine FBI background check required for appointment to the National Endowment for the Arts in 1963 prompted Straight to confess his Communist connections. He named Anthony Blunt and Guy Burgess as members of the Cambridge ring. Straight died in 2004 at the age of 87.

FROM PLATO'S RETREAT TO THE CIA

UM32 THE "SWINGING" KOECHERS

Residence at 50 East 89th Street

Playing the role of defectors from Czechoslovakia's repressive regime in 1965, Karl and Hana Koecher posed as passionate anti-Communists when meeting with their new American friends. In fact, both were active illegals and intelligence officers of the *Stanitajini Bezpecnost*–StB–the Czech intelligence service. With Karl studying at Columbia University, the couple resided at ***50 East 89th Street*** 32 in a luxury building with neighbors like Mel Brooks, Anne Bancroft, and Tommy Tune. While in New York, the Koechers built reputations as "swingers" by frequenting ***Plato's Retreat in the Ansonia Hotel at 230 West 74th Street.*** 33

Karl and Hana Koecher lived an American immigrant's dream in a New York high-rise in the Carnegie Hill section of Manhattan.

Hana is remembered as being "incredibly beautiful" as well as "sweet and ingratiating" and always the star of a party. The couple's multi-partner lifestyle enabled them to make contacts throughout a cross-section of similarly "open-minded, partner-swapping partygoers." They literally rubbed shoulders and other body parts with diplomats, military officers, and socialites who had potential intelligence value because of what they knew or the contacts they could make.

Karl Koecher became a U.S. citizen in 1971, and landed a job as a CIA translator two years later. Their "swingers" life continued in their new Washington home with an increasingly broader range of military, political, government, and civilian contacts. In the course of his CIA work, Karl acquired sufficient information—passed by the Czech service to Soviet counterintelligence—to identify and arrest Aleksandr Ogorodnik, a Soviet diplomat and CIA mole in Moscow. Ogorodnik, code named TRIGON, killed himself in 1977 while under interrogation by the KGB in Moscow. The Koechers remained untouched until 1984, when they were arrested hours before boarding a flight to Switzerland. Karl Koecher eventually pled guilty to espionage on behalf of Czechoslovakia and was jailed in the U.S. until he was swapped for Soviet dissident Anatoly Scharansky in February of 1986 and returned with his wife to Prague.

SPIES EVERYWHERE

UNITED NATIONS

Manhattan's East Side between 42nd and 48th Streets

The compound that houses the United Nations on *Manhattan's East Side between 42nd and 48th Streets* (34) and the scores of diplomatically accredited foreign consulates scattered throughout the city are centers of espionage activity. Even before the first UN building on the banks of the East River was complete, Soviet spies under UN cover were recruiting and handling agents. For example, Valentin Gubitchev handled State Department employee Judith Coplon from a temporary UN office at *1270 Sixth Avenue.* (23)

Diplomacy and espionage often intertwine. Since its planning stages, the United Nations has been a stage for recruitments, defections, and clandestine operations.

The presence of the UN enhanced New York's historic reputation as a hotbed of espionage, as diplomats from virtually every nation took up residence in the city. Amid its vibrant, ethnically diverse populations, a foreign accent arouses no suspicion. With hundreds of hotels, thousands of restaurants, scores of public parks, over 600 miles of subway, and round-the-clock activity, the city presents nearly unlimited options for surveillance detection routes, dead drops, signal sites, brief encounters, and clandestine meetings.

INSTRUCTIONS FOR NEW SOVIET SPIES IN NEW YORK SOMETIMES SOUNDED LIKE QUOTES FROM A TOURIST GUIDEBOOK.

During the Cold War, Soviet Bloc countries packed as many intelligence officers as possible into their UN missions under a variety of diplomatic and trade covers. New York became a highly desired posting for KGB and GRU officers, who were allocated funds to live well and entertain lavishly. Instructions for new Soviet spies in New York sometimes sounded like quotes from a tourist guidebook: "The existence of a subway in New York helps locating different places in the city," one Soviet advised new arrivals. "It should be borne in mind, however, that the system is quite complicated and should be studied carefully before planning to use it for operational purposes."

Social protocol was also important to the Soviets. "It is the practice in all restaurants to tip the waitress 10 percent of the amount shown on the check . . . It is not enough, for example, to ask, 'Give me a glass of beer.' It is also necessary to name the brand of beer ('Schlitz, Rheingold,' etc.)." Genuine Soviet diplomats grumbled to Moscow superiors that their "colleagues" were not only paid better, but also were allowed to slack off in performing their cover work.

Should an operation go bad, the UN offered an international forum to levy accusations and air grievances. After an American U-2 spy plane was shot down over the USSR in 1960, Soviet Premier Khrushchev used the event to create an international crisis, canceling a planned summit to embarrass President Eisenhower. Three weeks later, Henry Cabot Lodge, U.S. Ambassador to the UN, countered Khrushchev's grandstanding by displaying the bugged Great Seal of the United States that hung undetected in the American ambassador's Moscow office for six years after World War II.

Soviet Foreign Minister Andrei Gromyko responded with feigned indignation, telling the council that the U.S.'s accusations of widespread Soviet espionage were "more appropriate to the pages of a cheap detective novel than the security council."

The brief skirmish between the superpowers, fought with weapons of words on the UN battleground, made headlines around the world. Three years later, in 1963, the two countries swapped spies: American U-2 pilot Francis Gary Powers for Soviet illegal Rudolph Abel.

SPIES' FAVORITE SITES

THE KGB IN THE BRONX

David Marcus Movie Theater (originally Tuxedo Theater), 3464 Jerome Avenue

This Bronx theater became a preferred meeting location for Soviet intelligence officers and their spies during the Cold War.

When KGB Major Vasili Mitrokhin defected to the West in the early 1990s, he brought with him a treasure trove of notes copied during his three decades as a senior archivist for the Russian intelligence service. From those documents, Mitrokhin and Christopher Andrew wrote *The Sword and the Shield*, revealing decades of Soviet intelligence secrets.

Given the sensational nature of the text, it was easy to overlook a small appendix entitled *Some Favorite KGB Yavkas (Meeting Places) In the 1960s.* Included are dozens of specific meeting locations in America's largest cities favored by Soviet intelligence. Not surprisingly, New York City was repeatedly mentioned as an operational center. The KGB seemed to be particularly attracted to the Bronx. ***The David Marcus Movie Theater*** (originally the Tuxedo Theater) at ***3464 Jerome Avenue,*** 35 a favorite meeting place, is now the site of a U.S. post office. Another Bronx theater, the ***Earl Theatre, 58 East 161st Street,*** 36 now a Yankee Stadium–area sports bar, was also a popular Soviet meeting place in the 1940s. The "restaurant Savarin" was most likely part of the long-gone restaurant chain operated by the Union News Company with locations scattered throughout the city. Other operational sites identified were the "display window" of "Wilma's Party Center," most likely a small business that has since closed, and the awning of ***Middletown Inn Restaurant, 3188 Middletown Road,*** 37 which has been transformed into a suburban residential area.

OPERATION PANDORA

In an attempt to exploit racial divisions among Americans, the KGB planned to launch Operation Pandora in New York in 1971. Conceived by the KGB's First Directorate, the local *rezidentura* was to set off an explosive device in "the Negro section of New York." It is unclear whether this meant Harlem, parts of Brooklyn, or the Bronx, but an unnamed Moscow plotter suggested "one of the Negro colleges." According to the plan, the explosions would be followed by anonymous calls that blamed the terrorist act on the radical Jewish Defense League.

While the operation was never executed, that same year KGB chief Yuri Andropov approved the printing and U.S. distribution of racist pamphlets that looked as if they originated with the Jewish Defense League, while corresponding letters detailing Jewish atrocities against African Americans were sent to African American organizations. In the wake of the riots of the 1960s, these socially incendiary plots were produced in the hopes of creating "mass disorders in New York."

PERFECTING TRADECRAFT

BRUSH PASS IN GRAND CENTRAL STATION

15 Vanderbilt Avenue

Clandestine meetings with agents in countries behind the Iron Curtain presented challenging operational problems for CIA case officers during the Cold War. From Moscow to Prague to East Berlin, Soviet and Soviet-trained counterintelligence officers were vigilant, suspicious, and seemingly omnipresent. A pioneer in developing new tradecraft to defeat such pervasive security was a "denied-area" chief of station, Haviland Smith. After a Czech agent refused to use the standard dead drop method of covert communication out of fear of leaving the package unattended for any length of time, Smith began re-engineering the classic "brief encounter" technique of tradecraft called the *brush pass*. The brush pass is a rapidly executed handoff of a document or package between two persons in a public place that is done so quickly and naturally that it is virtually undetectable. Smith's innovation introduced elements of a magician's sleight of hand and misdirection into the maneuver, which he combined with careful site selection and precise choreography to effect the exchange. He developed the technique using the stairways and congestion of ***Grand Central Station at 15 Vanderbilt Avenue*** 38 during the 1960s and introduced it to a Czech agent along the walkway to the defunct Biltmore Hotel, now the Bank of America Plaza, near a subway stairway. Smith later demonstrated the new technique at a hotel in Washington, where agency veterans were unable to detect the clandestine handoff.

During the height of the Cold War, a CIA officer perfected new styles of clandestine brush passes in the crowded corridors of New York's historic train station.

PRIEST, SPY, AND MARRIED WITH CHILDREN

FATHER MARK CHEUNG

Church of the Transfiguration, 25 Mott Street

Larry Wu-Tai Chin's arrest in 1985 was a major embarrassment for the CIA. The retired analyst and translator spied for Communist China's Ministry for State Security (MSS) throughout his three-decade career at the agency. When confronted by the FBI, Wu-Tai Chin eventually admitted his contact with the Chinese Communists, but claimed he was only conducting personal shadow diplomacy to ease tensions between the U.S. and China. At the trial, prosecutors argued Wu-Tai Chin was motivated by profit. Evidence proved that he received hundreds of thousands of dollars for spying and used the money to buy rental properties and gamble in Las Vegas. In February 1986, the jury sentenced the sixty-three-year-old to two life sentences and fines of more than $3 million. Two weeks later, Chin suffocated himself with a plastic bag in an Alexandria, Virginia, jail cell.

Virtually lost in the Wu-Tai Chin drama was the abrupt departure of a beloved New York Roman Catholic priest, Father Mark Cheung, from his position at the ***Church of the Transfiguration, 25 Mott Street at Mosco Street,*** 39 in the heart of New York's Chinatown. Posted as an assistant pastor in 1972 to the landmark church—which sits on the notorious *Five Points* made famous in the movie *Gangs of New York*—Cheung had been promoted to parish administrator, but mysteriously vanished the day after Chin's arrest.

The Church of the Transfiguration, built in the early 1800s, unwittingly employed a Chinese spy who posed as a priest.

Secretly, Cheung had been working as an intelligence officer for China's MSS. He was responsible for providing emergency covert communications and an escape route for Chin in the event of discovery; one phase of the plan was to be initiated by a meeting in a confessional. Cheung's religious cover had been laboriously constructed over years and with previous postings at churches throughout the South Pacific. When the FBI eventually tracked down Cheung in Hong Kong, the priest-spy refused to answer questions and promptly disappeared into mainland China. Only later was it discovered that "Father Mark" was actually married with children.

SPYING ON ALLIES

ISRAEL'S NEW YORK CONSULATE

800 Second Avenue

The heavily guarded Israeli consulate served as the base for high-profile spy operations during the 1980s.

Jonathan Jay Pollard, an employee of the U.S. Naval Investigative Service, was recruited to spy in the 1980s by the Israeli Bureau of Scientific Relations, *ha-Lishka le-KishreiMada,* or LAKAM. In reality, LAKAM collected foreign scientific and technical intelligence and aggressively targeted potential agents, including U.S. citizens. Israeli Air Force Colonel Aviem Sella, operating from the *Israeli Consulate at 800 Second Avenue* 40 and undercover as a student of computer science at New York University, pitched Pollard, who readily agreed to cooperate. As a covert source, Pollard was assigned the code name THE HUNTING HORSE, meaning "someone who brings in good information that his superiors use to their own advantage."

Sella later handed Pollard off to another Israeli case officer, Yosef Yagur, who also worked out of the Second Avenue consulate. For more than a year, Pollard smuggled hundreds of thousands of pages of classified information from his office to his handlers in return for jewelry, trips, and a $2,500 monthly stipend. Arrested in 1985, he pled guilty to espionage and received a life sentence. LAKAM was disbanded in 1986, following Pollard's arrest. Israel formally acknowledged Pollard as its spy in 1998 and continues to press the U.S. government for his release.

Yagur also ran other American agents, such as Ben-Ami Kadish, who worked without compensation between 1979 and 1985 for Israeli intelligence, providing secret technical information on the Patriot missile system, F-15 fighter jets, and nuclear weapons. Arrested in 2008, the eighty-five-year-old Kadish pled guilty declaring he spied "for the benefit of Israel." In deference to his age, the spy received a $50,000 fine but no jail time. For its part, Israel's consulate general brushed aside the matter, saying, "[t]his is an old case which occurred over twenty-five years ago, and all aspects of it are part of the past."

ALWAYS A NEW YORKER

DCI WILLIAM CASEY

One of the CIA's most controversial directors was also the quintessential New Yorker. William Joseph Casey, who served as CIA director from 1981 to 1987, got his start in espionage during World War II working with Army intelligence and then the OSS as a protégé of William "Wild Bill" Donovan. Born in 1913 in the working- class neighborhood of Elmhurst, Queens, Casey attended public schools 13 and 89, received his undergraduate degree from Fordham University, and earned a law degree from St. John's University School of Law.

Following the war, he worked as a corporate lawyer while playing an active role in Republican politics and co-founding the conservative think tank, the Manhattan Institute. Casey then served as campaign manager for Ronald Reagan in 1980, before re-entering the world of espionage. Known inside the intelligence community for expanding the CIA's capabilities against Soviet and terrorist targets, he became embroiled in the Iran-Contra scandal during President Reagan's second term. Always the New Yorker, Casey was known to quip, "You know the best thing about Washington? It's only an hour to New York." While serving as DCI in December 1986, Casey became incapacitated by a brain tumor. He was never able to return to work and died the following May.

21st-CENTURY SPYING

The collapse of the Soviet Union did not diminish espionage activity in New York. Spies of all nationalities and ideologies, as well as terrorists, continue to call New York home. The bombing of the World Trade Building in 1993, the attacks on the Twin Towers in 2001, and the foiled Times Square bombing of 2010 reflect the changing nature of international conflict. While the ten Russian intelligence officers arrested in 2010–many of whom either lived in the city or were frequent visitors–may have evoked nostalgia in some Cold War warriors and intelligence historians, the lesson was clear: From the Revolutionary War of 1776 to present day, New York remains "a city of spies."

DINNER SERVED BY A FUTURE SPYMASTER

SCOBEE DINER

25229 Northern Boulevard, Little Neck, Queens

Open for more than seven decades as the Twentieth Century Diner and later as the Scobee Diner (closed in 2010), the landmark neighborhood eatery at *25229 Northern Boulevard, Little Neck, Queens* ❶ gave George Tenet, director of the Central Intelligence Agency (1997–2004), an early education in hard work. The family-owned diner was sold in the early 1960s, but Tenet's father stayed on as chef, and America's future spymaster bussed tables to earn the money to buy his first car. Tenet graduated from Benjamin N. Cardozo public high school in Bayside, Queens, and went on to earn degrees from Georgetown in Washington, D.C., and Columbia University. Although he would eventually enter the closemouthed intelligence profession, young George's reputation at the diner was that of a conversationalist who kept customers amused and returning. Among famous patrons who frequented the diner were the comedian Alan King and Telly "Kojak" Savalas.

AMONG FAMOUS PATRONS WHO FREQUENTED THE DINER WERE THE COMEDIAN ALAN KING AND TELLY "KOJAK" SAVALAS.

SUBWAY PHOTORECONNAISSANCE

IRANIAN SURVEILLANCE

Subway station, Roosevelt Avenue and 52nd Street, Queens

In 2003, a pair of Iranian diplomats was observed videotaping on the elevated subway station at *Roosevelt Avenue and 52nd Street in Queens* ❷ as the Manhattan-bound 7 train approached. It was 1:30 a.m. on a Sunday morning. Two uniformed police officers watched as the Iranians boarded the train and continued filming the train tracks from the front of the subway car. As the train approached the *Courthouse Square Station*, the cops moved in.

The men claimed they could not speak English, so a Farsi-speaking police officer interpreted. The pair identified themselves as diplomats assigned to Iran's UN mission at *622 Third Avenue* ❸ and claimed diplomatic immunity. They asserted they were returning from a party in Queens, but their camera contained only footage of subways.

In accordance with their diplomatic status, the alleged spies were not jailed but declared *persona non grata* and ordered out of the country. The episode was not the first expulsion for suspicious filming of New York by Iranian diplomats. A similar incident occurred in 2002, when two other Iranians connected to the UN were expelled for videotaping landmarks, including the Statue of Liberty, Brooklyn Bridge, and entrances to the tunnels leading to New Jersey.

IN ACCORDANCE WITH THEIR DIPLOMATIC STATUS, THE ALLEGED SPIES WERE NOT JAILED BUT DECLARED *PERSONA NON GRATA* AND ORDERED OUT OF THE COUNTRY.

More recently, Iran's government has been accused of using the Alavi Foundation, a nonprofit ostensibly devoted to charity work and promoting Islamic culture, as a front organization. The U.S. Attorney for the Southern District of New York filed a complaint that led to the seizure of Alavi's assets, including the Islamic Institute of New York, *55-11 Queens Boulevard, Woodside, Queens,* 4 the largest Shiite mosque in the city and the location most closely affiliated with Iran's UN mission.

FOMENTING TERROR

THE BLIND SHEIKH

Al-Farooq Mosque, 552 Atlantic Avenue, Brooklyn

Islamic radical Omar Abdel Rahman once led a storefront mosque on Brooklyn's Atlantic Avenue.

Before arriving in the United States, Islamic radical Omar Abdel Rahman was jailed in Egypt for alleged involvement in the 1981 assassination of Egyptian President Anwar Sadat. Eventually acquitted of the crime but expelled from the country, he relocated to New York in 1990. "The Blind Sheikh," as he became known, found an audience of disaffected immigrants in the small storefront *Al-Farooq Mosque at 552 Atlantic Avenue in Brooklyn.* 5

Rahman's message of hate reached a small number of disaffected Muslims who later carried out the attacks on the World Trade Center in 1993.

On February 26, 1993, a rented truck packed with 1,300 pounds of explosives blew up on parking level B-2 of the North Tower of the *New York World Trade Center,* 6 killing six people and injuring more than a thousand. The investigative trail uncovered Rahman's devastating plan to set off bombs in the Lincoln Tunnel, the Holland Tunnel, the United Nations, the Federal Plaza, and the George Washington Bridge. Arrested in June of 1993 with nine followers, Rahman was convicted in 1996 of seditious conspiracy and sentenced to life imprisonment. His attorney, Lynne F. Stewart, was subsequently disbarred and convicted of providing material aid to terrorism by smuggling messages to militant followers from her jailed client.

Despite the "Blind Sheikh's" conviction, the World Trade Center's Twin Towers remained an obsession for radical Islamic terrorists. On September 11, 2001, they struck again—crashing a civilian airliner into each of the buildings. The Twin Towers collapsed, causing collateral destruction to the World Trade Center's forty-seven-story original *Building 7 at 250 Greenwich Street,* 7 home to numerous government tenants, including the Department of Defense, the New York City Department of Emergency Management, the IRS, and the United States Secret Service. The Twin Towers are commemorated with a memorial at their previous location, while Building 7 was rebuilt in 2006 as a fifty-two-floor office structure.

The new 7 World Trade Center building was completed in 2006.

SPIES FOR FIDEL

CUBA'S UN MISSION

315 Lexington Avenue

The unassuming building of the permanent mission of Cuba to the United Nations at *315 Lexington Avenue* (8) attracts little notice from neighbors or passersby, but remains an active center for espionage. The Cuban handler of Ana Belen Montes, a senior Defense Intelligence Agency analyst who spied for Cuba from 1985 until her arrest in September of 2001, operated from the Lexington Avenue mission. Likewise, U.S. State Department official Walter Kendall Myers, code named AGENT 202 by the Cubans, and his wife, Gwendolyn Steingraber Myers, AGENT 123, were directed for some of their nearly thirty-year career of spying by Cuban intelligence officers assigned to the mission and operating under diplomatic immunity.

A small plaque at the front entrance on Lexington Avenue is the only indication this building serves as the Cuban Mission to the United Nations. Some of Cuba's most effective spies against the U.S. have been managed from here.

LM9

TRIPLE AGENT?

CHINA'S "PARLOR MAID"

137 Chrystie Street on the Lower East Side

Born in China, Katrina Leung (also known as Chen Wen Ying) immigrated to the U.S. in 1970 as a teenager. Living with an uncle in an apartment at ***137 Chrystie Street on the Lower East Side***, 9 she commuted to *Washington Irving High School at 40 Irving Place, near Gramercy Park*. Excelling at her studies, Leung received her undergraduate degree from Cornell University, and then followed her new husband to Chicago, where she received an MBA from the University of Chicago.

For a few years during childhood, Katrina Leung, codenamed Parlor Maid by the FBI, lived in New York.

Recruited by the FBI in the early 1980s (code name PARLOR MAID), she was known internally as *Bureau Source 410*. Tasked to spy on pro-mainland China groups in the Los Angeles area where she was living with her husband, Leung began an affair with her FBI handler a short time later. It was not long before she became a full-fledged U.S. citizen with the FBI's assistance. On her frequent business trips to China, she was allegedly recruited by the People's Republic of China's Ministry of State Security. Now said to be a double agent, code named LUO by the Chinese, she was reputed to increase the frequency of her China trips, contacts, and business dealings. In the late 1980s, she began an affair with yet another FBI special agent. Suspicions were raised in the early 1990s after her unreported contacts with Chinese intelligence were discovered, but the damage was contained when her FBI handler and lover conducted the investigation.

However, by 2001, suspicions were again raised and Leung became the target of a full FBI counterintelligence investigation. Somewhere along the way, Leung allegedly moved from double to triple agent. Accused of copying classified documents from her FBI lover's briefcase and passing them to her Chinese handler (code name MAO), she was arrested in 2003. The case dragged on until 2005, when, despite ample evidence of espionage, the judge dismissed the case after learning that the FBI agent's plea agreement with the government specified he "could not share further information relating to the case with Leung or her counsel." Without the opportunity to depose the agent as a witness, Leung would have been denied her right to a fair trial. Nevertheless, the loss of the classified information Leung allegedly passed to China is considered grave.

MONEY FOR ASSASSINS

PAYONEER CORPORATION

410 Park Avenue

There could be little doubt that well-trained, organized professionals killed Palestinian militant Mahmoud al-Mabhouh in his room at Dubai's luxury Al Bustan Hotel in January 2010. According to Dubai authorities, images of twenty-seven members of the hit squad were captured on closed-circuit television in and around the hotel. Who was behind the killing? One law enforcement officer in Dubai is quoted as saying investigators are 99% certain the action was carried out by Israel's intelligence service, Mossad. This is hardly a surprising conclusion considering al-Mabhouh's history of organizing terror attacks against Israel. But is there evidence of a New York City connection?

A virtual office in this Park Avenue building served as headquarters for Payoneer, an Internet-based financial services company.

Examination of financial and credit card records of the assassins led investigators back to a New York company, Payoneer, with an address at *410 Park Avenue*. 10 Run by an Israeli named Yuval Tal, the firm provides prepaid debit MasterCards to companies who use them to pay employee travel expenses or contractors. Investigators determined that fourteen of the suspected assassins used prepaid Payoneer cards for hotel rooms and travel. Tal himself is reputed to have been a former member of Israeli special forces. However, when a journalist researching the story went to Payoneer's Park Avenue suite, he found only a virtual office that handled the phones and mail for hundreds of firms. The real Payoneer is located at an undisclosed address.

GHOST STORIES

A NEW GENERATION OF RUSSIAN ILLEGALS

Anna Chapman Residence, 20 Exchange Place

When the FBI rolled up ten Russian intelligence officers in June of 2010, the story made international headlines. Those arrested were part of a long-running Russian *Sluzhba Vneshney Razvedki (SVR)* illegals operation that reached from Boston into New York, New Jersey, Northern Virginia, and west to Seattle. The reaction, both in the media and among the public, was more a sense of amusement than alarm, as if the episode was a chapter from a Cold War novel. The Russian Foreign Ministry's response played

WHEN RUSSIAN ILLEGALS VLADIMIR GURYEV (ALIAS RICHARD MURPHY) AND MIKHAIL KUSTIK (ALIAS MICHAEL ZOTTOLI) MET FOR THE FIRST TIME, IT WAS BENEATH THE GLOBE ADORNING THE NORTH SIDE OF COLOMBUS CIRCLE ON JUNE 20, 2004. THE VERBAL PAROLE (CODE PHRASE) WAS "UNCLE PAUL SENDS HIS LOVE." THEY THEN MOVED THE MEETING TO A MORE PRIVATE LOCATION.

a similar tune: "We don't understand the reasons which prompted the U.S. Department of Justice to make a public statement in the spirit of Cold Wa-era spy stories."

New York City and its surrounding areas were hubs for the spy operations that ran for more than a decade. Clandestine meetings for transferring cash, supplies, and information occurred at sites from downtown Brooklyn to the Globe sculpture outside the *Trump International Hotel and Tower at One Central Park West* and the adjoining ***Columbus***

Spies met near easily identified landmarks such as the Globe at Columbus Circle. They then moved their meeting to a more private location.

Circle. 11 Anna Chapman, the youngest of the intelligence officers, used a range of sites including a ***Starbucks on 47th Street and Eighth Avenue*** 12 and the ***Barnes & Noble Bookstore, 97 Warren Street in Tribeca*** 13 to communicate with her Russian handlers via special software on her laptop computer.

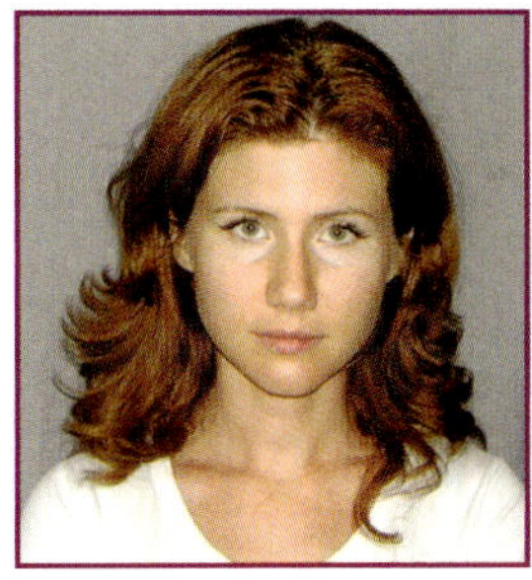

Russian spy Anna Vasil'evna Kushchenko, better known as Anna Chapman, met with an undercover FBI special agent posing as a Russian intelligence officer at the Starbucks on Hanover Square.

Russian illegal Mikhail A. Vasenkov, alias Juan Lazaro.

Vicky Peláez, a U.S. citizen from Peru, and Mikhail A. Vasenkov, living under the alias of Juan Lazaro at *17 Clifton Avenue in Yonkers* 14 since 1985, commuted into New York for their cover jobs. A self-described "journalist and anthropologist," Lazaro secretly retired from the SVR in 2006 after an intelligence career of three decades. Vicky Peláez wrote columns critical of American policy for the left-leaning Spanish language paper, *El Diario La Prensa*, now located on the *18th floor of One MetroTech Center, Brooklyn*. 15

Vladimir and Lidiya Guryev, using aliases Richard and Cynthia Murphy, lived in Montclair, New Jersey, in a $481,000 house paid for by their Moscow controllers. Lidiya commuted into the city for a job as a vice president of a small wealth management firm, Morea Financial Services, at *120 Broadway.*

(14) In the U.S. since the mid-1990s, Lidiya earned degrees from New York University and an MBA from Columbia Business School. Guryev (Richard Murphy) playing the role of a "house husband," met with his handlers in New York City as well as abroad, and transferred money and spy gear to another illegal couple, Mikhail Kutsik and Natalia Pereverzeva (Michael Zottoli and Patricia Mills). As recently as March 7 of 2010, Guryev passed an updated laptop, money, and encrypted flash media cards to Kutsik at the now defunct ***Tillie's Coffee Shop at 248 Dekalb Avenue*** (16) in Brooklyn's hip Fort Greene neighborhood.

Of the ten illegals, media attention focused on the photogenic Anna Kushchenko Chapman, who lived on the 52nd floor in a fashionable Financial District high-rise at ***20 Exchange Place.*** (17) The 28-year-old redhead established cover as an Internet real estate entrepreneur. Just prior to her meeting with an FBI undercover agent in the ***Starbucks at 10 Hanover Place*** (18) and subsequent arrest on June 27, 2010, at the ***1st Precinct, 16 Ericsson Place*** (19), she became CEO of a start-up company, PropertyFinder LLC, and purchased the web site, www.NYCrentals.com.

Originally headquarters for the City Bank Farmers Trust Company, this fifty-seven-story art deco masterpiece was home to spy Anna Chapman. Befitting her cover as a young fashion-forward professional, Chapman was among the first wave of residents to move into these Financial District apartments.

Responsible for one of the NYPD's smallest precincts, the 1st Precinct gained prominence as the location where Russian spy Anna Chapman surrendered her passport and was arrested.

Leading a high-flying lifestyle, Chapman posed for pictures for society photographers, associated with celebrities at parties, frequented trendy nightspots, and maintained updated profiles on Facebook and LinkedIn. Once London tabloids obtained semi-nude photographs of Chapman, she became internationally known as "the hot spy." Compared to the other nine low-key Russian spies, she projected all the glamour of a Hollywood-scripted secret agent. Chapman's "Bond Girl"–meets–"Sex and the City" story overshadowed the national security threat posed by the Moscow-directed spy network.

After the ten were returned to Russia as part of spy swap, Chapman evolved into a national hero with her own television show, *Secrets of the World with Anna Chapman*. Her provocative poses graced the pages of *Maxim* magazine and she paraded down the catwalk during fashion week in Moscow, accidentally dropping the real pistol she carried as a prop. The Russian intelligence failure inadvertently

LEADING A HIGH-FLYING LIFESTYLE, CHAPMAN POSED FOR PICTURES FOR SOCIETY PHOTOGRAPHERS, ASSOCIATED WITH CELEBRITIES AT PARTIES, FREQUENTED TRENDY NIGHTSPOTS, AND MAINTAINED UPDATED PROFILES ON FACEBOOK AND LINKEDIN.

produced a pop culture star and a youthful new image for the SVR. Chapman appeared a world apart from the dour Soviet Cold War spies whose only public recognition might be a colorless commemorative postage stamp.

The image-conscious Vladimir Putin seized the opportunity to minimize the importance of the ten intelligence officers and underplay the significance of their arrests. Appearing on *Larry King Live* on December 1, 2010, Putin admitted they were spies, but asserted they would have only become operational "in crisis periods, say, in case of a breakup of the diplomatic relations." In other words, the ten were spies, but as "sleeper agents" posed no security threats to the United States.

The reality was otherwise. All of the illegals were dedicated, trained officers of the SVR, Russia's successor to the KGB's First Directorate. Except for Chapman and another young officer, Mikhail Semenko, all were seasoned, extensively trained intelligence officers. An encrypted memo from Moscow to the Murphys, intercepted by the FBI, clarified their mission: "You were sent to U.S.A for long-term service trip. Your education, bank accounts, car, house etc.–all these serve one goal: fulfill your main mission, i.e. to search and develop ties in policymaking circles in U.S. and send [intelligence reports] to the Center."

The decade-long FBI operation that exposed the Russian spies, code named GHOST STORIES, involved hundreds of agents and thousands of hours of manpower. The investigation uncovered a sophisticated and far-ranging intelligence operation that integrated traditional tradecraft with the latest advancements in communications technology. The Russian spies used private *ad hoc* wireless networks to burst data from laptops to mobile units, executed "flash-passes" in train stations to exchange money, and employed steganography to embed encrypted messages in images of flowers posted to sites on the Internet. Contrary to press narratives, the spies' levels of tradecraft sophistication and successes in developing access to influential members of America's financial and political community posed a serious and mounting threat to U.S. interests. Chapman particularly demonstrated that the effectiveness of *sexspionage* continues. A 21st century Mata Hari, she employed sex appeal to spot and ensnare wealthy and influential men in business and government for potential recruitment and exploitation by her intelligence service.

The FBI management of the GHOST STORIES operation required leadership, vision, discipline, security, patience, and perseverance. The ripples from the arrests have spread to expose additional SVR illegals in other parts of the world and the case has become one of the FBI's greatest counterintelligence successes.

SPYCATCHERS

THE NEW YORK FBI

Jacob K. Javits Federal Building, 26 Federal Plaza

The Federal Bureau of Investigation's history in New York dates to 1910. Two years after the FBI was established in Washington, D.C., the New York office opened in the Old Post Office Building, the site of what is now *City Hall Park*. Over the next four decades, the office moved to *15 Park Row*, to the *Subtreasury Building at Wall Street and Nassau Street, to 370 Lexington Avenue, to the Courthouse at Foley Square,* and then to *290 Broadway* in 1952, and to *201 East 69th Street* in 1956. Since 1980, the FBI New York field office has been at the ***Jacob K. Javits Federal Building, 26 Federal Plaza.*** 20 Through all the moves, the New York field office–the Bureau's largest, referred to as "the Anthill"–led the investigations into and arrests of some of the most famous foreign spies, spy rings, and terrorists in American history.

Called "The Ant Hill," the Jacob K. Javits Federal Building houses multiple government agencies, bureaus, and departments, including the FBI's largest field office. From here, agents have broken some of the most widely publicized espionage cases in the nation's history.

GLOSSARY

Abwehr–Germany's military intelligence agency from 1921 to 1944.

Access Agent–A person who facilitates contact with a target individual, group, or entry into a facility.

Agent–An individual, typically a foreign national, working clandestinely for an intelligence service.

Alias–A false identity used to protect an intelligence officer's true name. A false identity may be as simple as false business cards or it can include detailed background information and legitimate documentation.

Backstop–The use of references, documents (genuine or forged), legal papers, web presence, and social media to attest to an identity.

Brief Encounter–A planned, but seemingly random, passing of two individuals in a public location to clandestinely exchange documents or materials.

British Security Coordination (BSC)–The U.S.-based organization for British intelligence during World War II. BSC used the British Passport Control Office in Rockefeller Center as its cover.

Brush Pass or Flash Pass–The difficult-to-detect exchange of materials, such as documents, film, money, or other items during a brief encounter between an agent and case officer, typically in a public place. A brush pass usually occurs with no spoken communication, but if the participants are unknown to each other, it may involve a brief verbal parole or a recognition signal, such as wearing a baseball cap of a designated color.

BSC–See British Security Coordination.

Case–The official record of an intelligence operation.

Case Officer (also Operations Officer)–An intelligence officer responsible for an agent operation. Responsibilities may include recruitment and instruction, as well as those of paymaster and personal advisor.

CIA–Central Intelligence Agency.

Cipher–A method of cryptography (secret codes) that replaces a letter for a number or number for a letter. An extremely simple cipher might replace the letter "A" with a number "1," the letter "B" with a number "2" and so on. A more complex method of cryptography uses the transposition of letters or numbers. For example, the word "Agent" might become "Tegan."

Code–A method of cryptography similar to a cipher that converts letters, words, phrases, colors, or gestures into another form, but not necessarily of the same type. For example: a short code of three numbers may convert to a lengthy prearranged set of instructions.

Codebooks–A book that contains the "key" (instructions) for decoding either a cipher or code.

Code-breaking–The discipline of revealing the true meaning behind a coded message by use of mathematics, logic, or special software.

Code Name–An alias name, or cover name, for a person or operation for purposes of security.

Commercial Cover–A seemingly legitimate business that also includes an espionage component and/or personnel. A commercial cover may involve a business-to-business organization, a retail establishment open to the public, or a single individual operating undercover as a "consultant."

Concealment Device (CD)–An object modified or fabricated to contain either a device or intelligence materials for purposes of covert storage, transport, placement within a target, or "dead dropping."

Counterintelligence–Operations and analysis undertaken to identify and thwart penetrations of information systems, personnel, equipment, and installations by a foreign intelligence service.

Courier–A messenger in a clandestine operation.

Cover–An affiliation (relationship) used by a person, organization, or installation to mask their association with an intelligence service.

Covert Communication (Covcom)–Any technique or device used to relay data clandestinely from case officer to agent or agent to case officer.

CPUSA–Communist Party United States of America.

Cryptanalysis–The process by which coded messages are rendered understandable without benefit of the code's key.

Cutout–A non-alerting, sometimes unwitting, individual used to communicate between two or more persons engaged in an intelligence operation. For instance, a cutout may deliver messages between a case officer and an agent when the two cannot otherwise meet securely.

DCI–Director of Central Intelligence.

Dead Drop–A method of communication between an agent and handler in which materials or devices are left in a preselected location, typically in some form of concealment. A dead-dropped package may either be hidden or placed in the open in a concealment that either blends in with the surroundings and/or discourages close inspection by passersby. Dead drops separate the agent and handler by time, though not by location.

Decrypt–To break the code with or without use of a key.

Defector–A person who switches alliances from his or her home country to provide information to a foreign intelligence service. A "defector in place" will continue living in his or her home country while spying for a foreign intelligence service.

Diplomatic Cover–An intelligence officer identified and accredited as a member of a nation's diplomatic corps and afforded commensurate rights and privileges such as diplomatic immunity. In almost all instances, the diplomat's role as an intelligence officer is undisclosed to the host country.

Double Agent–An agent pretending to work on behalf of one intelligence service but, in reality, directed by a second service against the former.

Front Company–see Commercial Cover.

GRU (Glavnoye Razvedyvatelnoye Upravleine or Chief Intelligence Directorate of the General Staff)–Soviet and later Russian military intelligence service. Unlike the KGB (and successor organizations) the GRU is involved solely in foreign intelligence collection with no internal security component.

Handler–An individual, usually a case officer, who controls and directs an agent.

Illegal–The term used for Soviet and Russian intelligence officers operating abroad, usually in assumed identities, without diplomatic cover. Illegals pose as legitimate residents of the target country.

Invisible Ink–A chemical compound that when dissolved and used as ink renders writing on paper undetectable until reactivated by heat or another chemical called a "reagent." A centuries-old form of tradecraft, early forms of invisible ink included lemon juice as well as a combination of milk, sugar, and water.

KGB (Komitet Gosudarstvennoy Bezopasnosti or Committee for State Security)–The Soviet Union's primary security and intelligence organization responsible for internal as well as foreign intelligence gathering. It has gone through numerous iterations over the years, including Cheka, NKVD, and OGPU, among others.

MKULTRA–A top secret CIA program from 1953 to 1962 focused on researching the behavioral effects of drugs, alcohol, and other chemicals, including the newly discovered LSD, on human subjects.

Moscow Centre or Centre–Russian foreign intelligence headquarters in Moscow.

Mossad (HaMossad leModi'in uleTafkidim)–Israel's intelligence service.

MSS–The People's Republic of China's Ministry of State Security, which includes both the internal security service and the largest foreign intelligence service.

NKVD (Narodnyy Komisariat Vnutrennikh Del or The People's Commisariat for Internal Affairs)–Soviet intelligence service 1934–1946, forerunner of the KGB.

OGPU (Ob'edinyonnoye Gosudarstvennoye Politicheskoye Upravleniye or Unified State Political Administration)–Soviet Intelligence Service, forerunner to the NKVD from 1922 to 1934.

Office of Strategic Services (OSS)–America's World War II intelligence organization from 1942 to 1945.

Parole–Term for an exchange of prearranged words, phrases, or actions to confirm identity of intelligence operatives meeting for the first time. Paroles are designed to sound like common conversation.

Principal Agent–An agent responsible for handling or directing subordinate agents.

Recruiter–One who concludes an agreement with another person to commit espionage.

Recruitment–The process or act of enlisting a potential agent to spy.

Secret Ink–See Invisible Ink.

Secret Writing–A form of steganography that uses invisible ink (wet or dry) or microphotography to create a secret message that is embedded in a non-alerting letter or other carrier.

Sharashka–A prison in the Soviet Union built around a laboratory in which scientists with valuable knowledge or expertise were held in dormitory-like conditions to work on important projects–many of them secret.

Signal Site–A covert means of communication using a non-alerting signal, such as a chalk mark on a lamppost, to either initiate or terminate a clandestine act.

Spotting or Spotter–The act or person who identifies an individual with potential for spying. Spotters assess others for ideology, specific talents, access to secrets, weaknesses, and psychological vulnerabilities.

Spy–An individual who obtains secrets on behalf of a foreign intelligence service.

Spycatcher–A counterintelligence professional.

Spymaster–Term usually applied to the head of an intelligence organization or a senior intelligence officer.

Spy Network or Spy Ring–A group of spies usually directed toward a common objective by a single handler.

Stay-Behind Agent–A spy who remains in place following occupation by an enemy force.

Stub (Štátna bezpe nos)–The former Czechoslovakia's secret intelligence service, 1945–1990.

Surveillance Detection Run/Route (SDR)–A planned route taken by an agent or handler prior to conducting a clandestine act in hostile territory designed to identify or elude surveillance.

SVR (Sluzhba Vneshney Razvedki)–Russia's foreign intelligence service, successor of the KGB's First Chief Directorate.

SWP–Socialist Workers Party.

Tradecraft–The techniques, technologies, and methodologies used in covert intelligence operations. Tradecraft applies to both the procedures, such as surveillance detection routes, as well as the use of devices and agent communications.

Undercover (Under cover)–Operations conducted using a false identity. A cover identity can last from a few hours to several years, depending on the operation.

VENONA–The code name for a code-breaking operation targeting Soviet secure communications intercepted between 1942 and 1945. The decrypts began in 1946 and continued until 1980. One of the most secretive operations of the Cold War, the existence of VENONA wasn't made public until the mid-1990s.

INDEX

GREENWICH VILLAGE
EAST VILLAGE
NOHO
SOHO
LITTLE ITALY
BOWERY
LOWER EAST SIDE
CHINATOWN
Ukranian Museum
St Marks Church
Cooper Union Landmark
Tompkins Square
Hamilton Fish Park
Sarah D Roosevelt Pkwy
Tenement Museum
Seward Park
Rutgers Park
Chinese History Museum
Columbus Park
Foley Square
Washington Square
New York University
New Museum of Contemporary Art
Alternative Museum
NYC Fire Museum
Walker Park
E 13th St
E 12th St
E 11th St
E 10th St
E 9th St
E 8th St
E 7th St
E 6th St
E 5th St
E 4th St
E 3rd St
E 2nd St
E 1st St
E Houston St
Szold Pl
Avenue D
Avenue C
Avenue B
Avenue A
Sheriff St
Pitt St
Ridge St
Attorney St
Clinton St
Suffolk St
Norfolk St
Essex St
Ludlow St
Orchard St
Allen St
Stanton St
Rivington St
Delancey St
Broome St
Eldridge St
Forsyth St
Chrystie St
Bowery
Freeman Al
Willett St
Samuel Dickstein Plz
Cherry St
Jefferson St
Rutgers St
Rutgers Slip
South St
Canal St
Pike St
E Broadway
Hester St
Madison St
Division St
Dovers St
Chatham Sq
Pell St
Bayard St
Mosco
Baxter St
Hamill Pl
Centre St
Benson St
Catherine Ln
Worth St
Thomas St
Leonard St
Franklin St
Franklin Pl
White St
Walker St
Lispenard St
Church St
Cortlandt Aly
Howard St
Grand St
Centre Market Pl
Kenmare St
Cleveland Pl
Lafayette St
Mulberry St
Mott St
Elizabeth St
Extra Pl
Jersey St
Crosby St
Broadway
Mercer St
Greene St
Wooster St
W Broadway
Prince St
Spring St
Thompson St
Sullivan St
Laguardia Pl
Watts St
Dominick St
Avenue Of The Americas
Varick St
Saint Johns Ln
York St
Beach St
N Moore St
Collister St
Hubert St
Laight St
Vestry St
Desbrosses St
Renwick St
Vandam St
Charlton St
King St
Hudson St
West St
Harrison St
Jay St
Staple St
Stuyvesant Al
Stuyvesant St
Taras Shevchenko Pl
Cooper Sq
Great Jones St
Great Jones Al
Bond St
Shinbone Al
Lafayette Ct
4th Ave
Astor Pl
Saint Marks Pl
Waverly Pl
Washington Pl
W 4th St
8th St
E 9th St
University Pl
Washington Sq E
Washington Mews
Macdougal Aly
Washington Sq N
Washington Sq S
Washington Sq W
W 3rd St
Minetta Ln
Minetta St
Macdougal St
Bedford St
Downing St
Carmine St
Cornelia St
Jones St
Leroy St
Commerce St
Grove St
Bleecker St
7th Ave S
Saint Lukes Pl
Gay St
W 8th St
W 9th St
Patchin Pl
W 10th St
Greenwich Ave
Charles St
Perry St
W 4th St
Greenwich St

Governors Island
Support Center
4

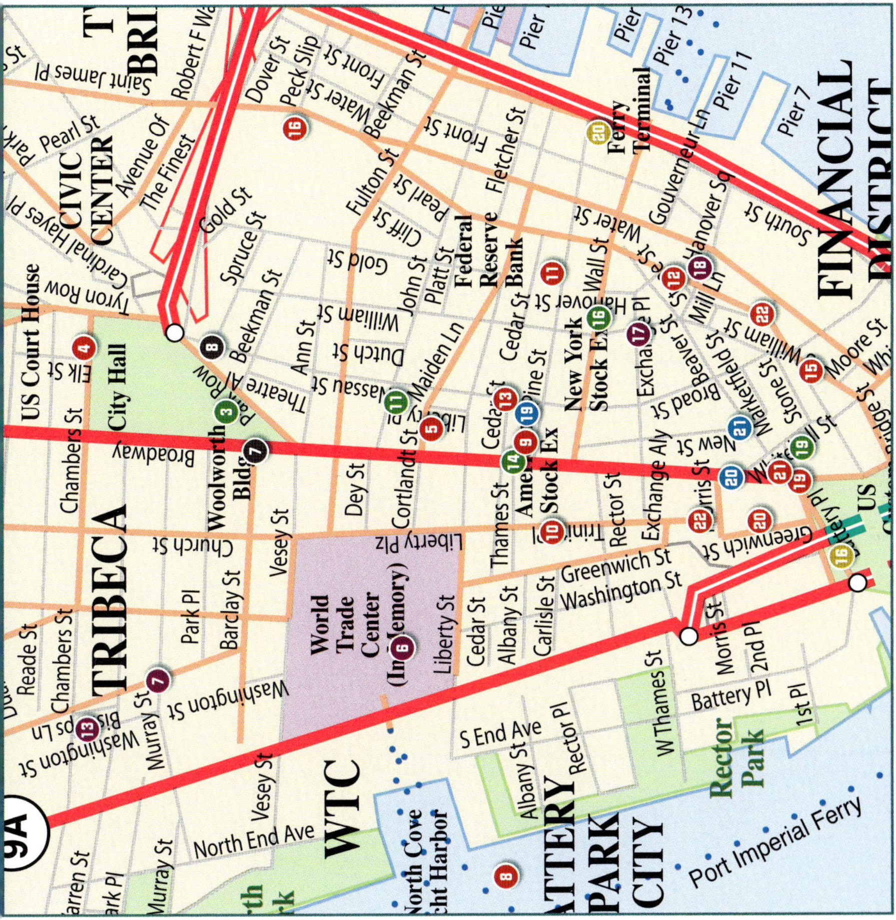

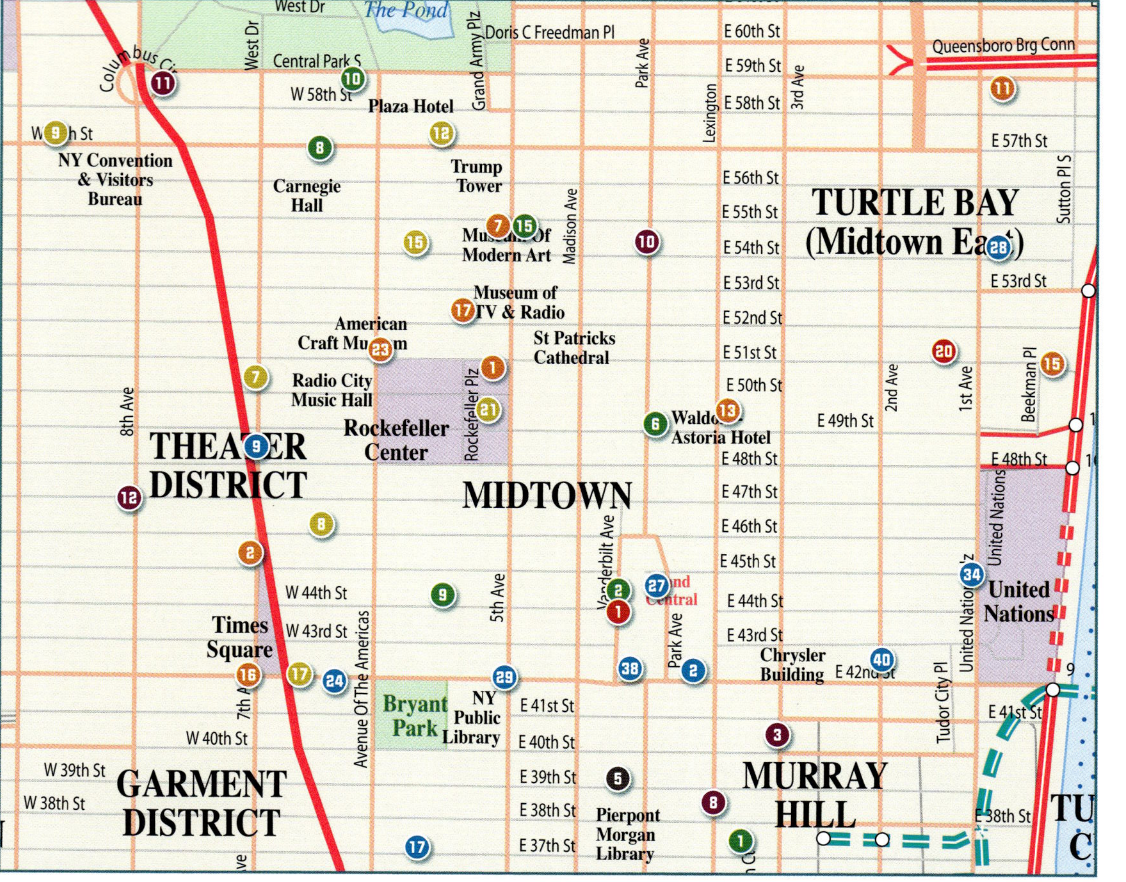

TURTLE BAY
(Midtown East)
MIDTOWN
THEATER DISTRICT
GARMENT DISTRICT
MURRAY HILL
United Nations
Chrysler Building
Waldorf Astoria Hotel
St Patricks Cathedral
Museum of TV & Radio
Museum of Modern Art
Trump Tower
Plaza Hotel
Carnegie Hall
American Craft Museum
Radio City Music Hall
Rockefeller Center
Times Square
NY Public Library
Bryant Park
Pierpont Morgan Library
NY Convention & Visitors Bureau
The Pond
West Dr
Central Park S
Grand Army Plz
Doris C Freedman Pl
Columbus Cir
Queensboro Brg Conn
Sutton Pl S
Beekman Pl
Tudor City Pl
United Nations Plz
Rockefeller Plz
Vanderbilt Ave
Park Ave
Lexington
Madison Ave
5th Ave
Avenue Of The Americas
7th Ave
8th Ave
3rd Ave
2nd Ave
1st Ave
E 60th St
E 59th St
E 58th St
E 57th St
E 56th St
E 55th St
E 54th St
E 53rd St
E 52nd St
E 51st St
E 50th St
E 49th St
E 48th St
E 47th St
E 46th St
E 45th St
E 44th St
E 43rd St
E 42nd St
E 41st St
E 40th St
E 39th St
E 38th St
E 37th St
W 58th St
W 44th St
W 43rd St
W 40th St
W 39th St
W 38th St

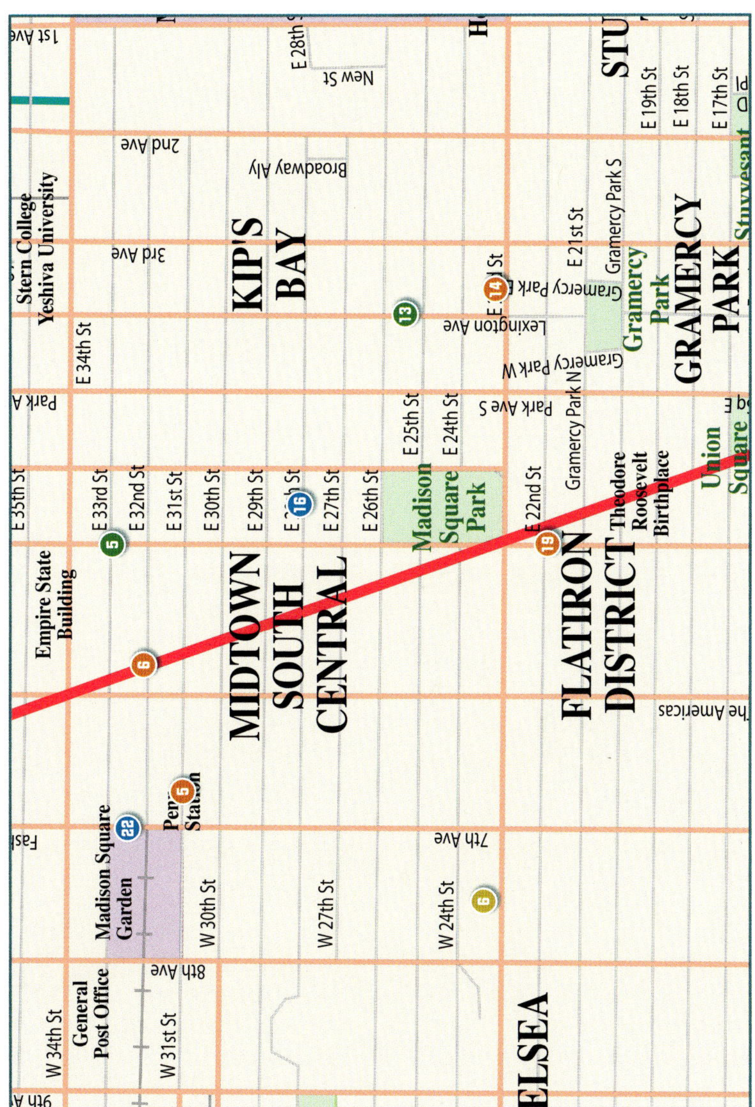
MIDTOWN SOUTH CENTRAL
KIP'S BAY
FLATIRON DISTRICT
GRAMERCY PARK
Empire State Building
Stern College Yeshiva University
Madison Square Garden
General Post Office
Madison Square Park
Gramercy Park
Theodore Roosevelt Birthplace
Union Square
W 34th St
W 31st St
W 30th St
W 27th St
W 24th St
E 35th St
E 34th St
E 33rd St
E 32nd St
E 31st St
E 30th St
E 29th St
E 27th St
E 26th St
E 25th St
E 24th St
E 22nd St
E 21st St
E 19th St
E 18th St
E 17th St
New St
Broadway Aly
Gramercy Park S
Gramercy Park W
Gramercy Park N
Park Ave S
Lexington Ave
3rd Ave
2nd Ave
7th Ave
8th Ave

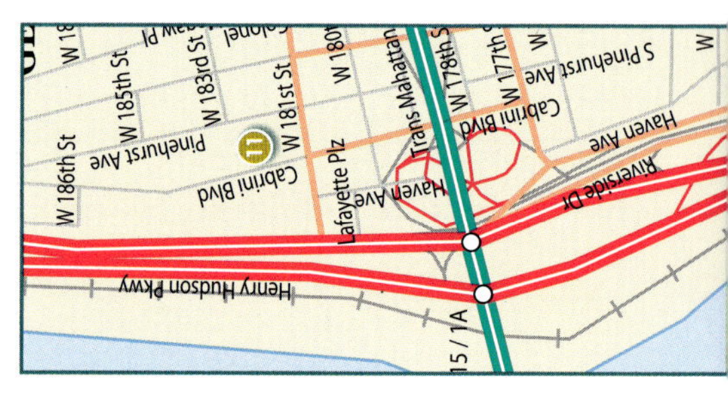

HEIGHTS (Sugar Hill)

Hamilton Grange Natl Mon

City University of New York

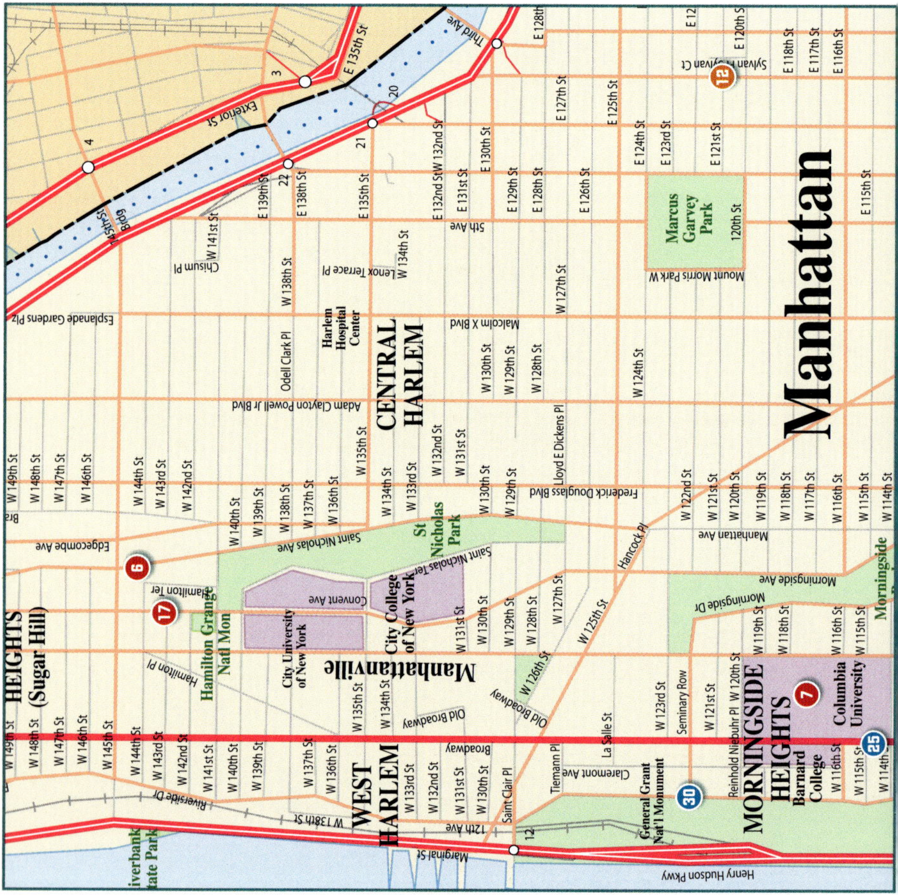

City College of New York

Manhattanville

St Nicholas Park

WEST HARLEM

CENTRAL HARLEM

Harlem Hospital Center

Marcus Garvey Park

Manhattan

MORNINGSIDE HEIGHTS

Barnard College

Columbia University

General Grant Nat'l Monument

UPPER WEST SIDE
LINCOLN SQUARE
UPPER EAST SIDE
YORKVILLE
LENOX HILL
ROOSEVELT ISLAND
East River
Ferry Terminal
Carl Schurz Park
Gracie Mansion
Gracie Sq
Gracie Ter
Henderson Pl
John Jay Park
Cherokee Pl
Cornell Medical College
New York Hospital Center
Rockefeller University
Abigail Adams Smith House Museum
Queensboro Brdg
Queensboro Brg Conn
E 34th St - E 90th St
Fdr Dr
York Ave
First Ave
Second Ave
Third Ave
Lexington Ave
Park Ave
Madison
5th Ave
Jewish Museum
Cooper Hewitt Museum
James Cagney Pl
Whitney Museum of American Art
Asia Soci Museum
City University of New York
Main St
Central Rd N
River Rd
West Rd
East Rd
Road 10
Road 6
Road 5
Courts
The Reservoir
86th St Transverse Rd
Central Park
Great Lawn
Metropolitan Museum Of Art
Metropolitan Museum Parking Dr
Delecorte Theater
Belvedere Lake
Obelisk
Belvedere Castle
79th St Transverse Rd
The Ramble
Boat House
The Lake
Bethesda Fountain & Terrace
East Dr
Conservatory Pond
Cherry Hill
72nd Street Traverse
Bandshell
The Frick Collection
Sheep Meadow
The Mall
Tavern On The Green
65th Street Transverse Rd
Zoo
The Dairy
Center Dr
Heckscher Playground
Wollman Rink
The Pond
West Dr
Central Park S
Grand Army Plz
Doris C Freedman
Plaza Hotel
Columbus Cir
Central Park W
Columbus Ave
Broadway
W End Ave
Amsterdam
Pomander Walk
Children's Museum
Hayden Planetarium
American Museum Of Natural Histor
York Historical Society
Pharmacy College
Museum of American Folk Art
Julliard School
Lincoln Center
Harkness Plz
NY State Theater
Damrosch Park
Fordham Univ
Freedom Pl

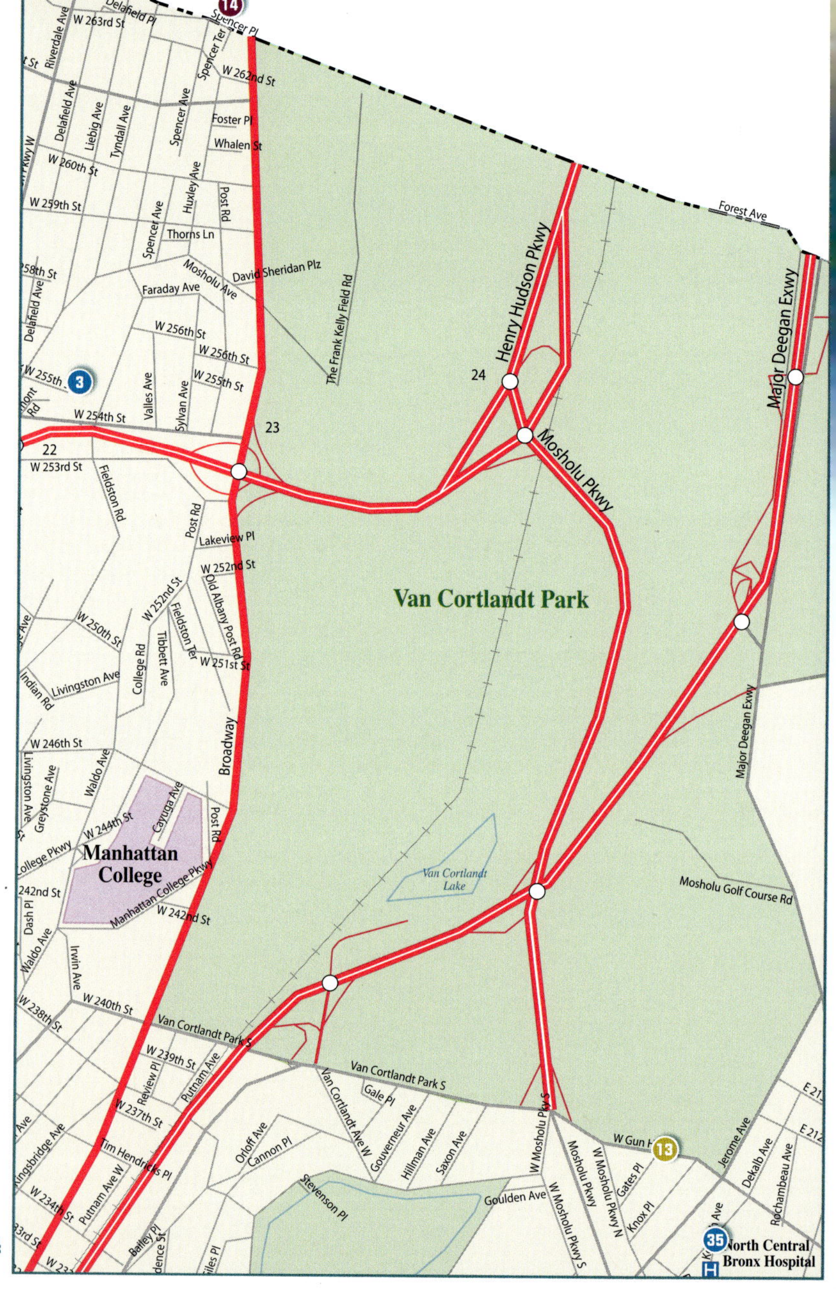

N
Van Cortlandt Park
Manhattan College
Van Cortlandt Lake
North Central Bronx Hospital
Henry Hudson Pkwy
Mosholu Pkwy
Major Deegan Exwy
Broadway
The Frank Kelly Field Rd
Mosholu Golf Course Rd
Van Cortlandt Park S
Forest Ave
Delafield Pl
W 263rd St
Spencer Pl
Spencer Ter
W 262nd St
Riverdale Ave
Delafield Ave
Liebig Ave
Tyndall Ave
Spencer Ave
Foster Pl
Whalen St
W 260th St
W 259th St
Huxley Ave
Post Rd
Thorns Ln
Mosholu Ave
David Sheridan Plz
Faraday Ave
W 256th St
W 255th St
W 254th St
Valles Ave
Sylvan Ave
W 253rd St
Fieldston Rd
Lakeview Pl
W 252nd St
Old Albany Post Rd
Fieldston Ter
Tibbett Ave
W 251st St
W 250th St
College Rd
Livingston Ave
Indian Rd
W 246th St
Waldo Ave
Greystone Ave
Cayuga Ave
W 244th St
College Pkwy
Manhattan College Pkwy
W 242nd St
242nd St
Dash Pl
Irwin Ave
W 240th St
W 238th St
W 239th St
Review Pl
Putnam Ave
W 237th St
Tim Hendricks Pl
Kingsbridge Ave
Putnam Ave W
W 234th St
Bailey Pl
Orloff Ave
Cannon Pl
Stevenson Pl
Van Cortlandt Ave W
Gale Pl
Gouverneur Ave
Hillman Ave
Saxon Ave
Goulden Ave
W Mosholu Pkwy S
Mosholu Pkwy
W Mosholu Pkwy N
Gates Pl
Knox Pl
Jerome Ave
Dekalb Ave
Rochambeau Ave
W Gun H
22
23
24
3
13
14
35

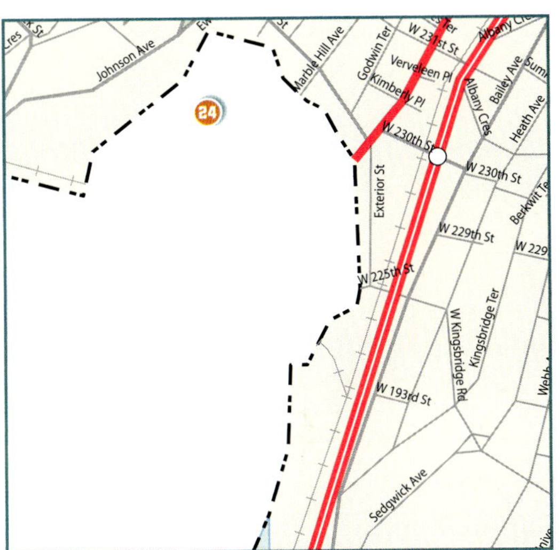
Johnson Ave
Marble Hill Ave
Godwin Ter
W 231st St
Albany Cres
Verveleen Pl
Kimberly Pl
Bailey Ave
Heath Ave
W 230th St
W 230th St
Exterior St
Berkwit Ter
W 229th St
W 225th St
W Kingsbridge Rd
Kingsbridge Ter
W 193rd St
Sedgwick Ave

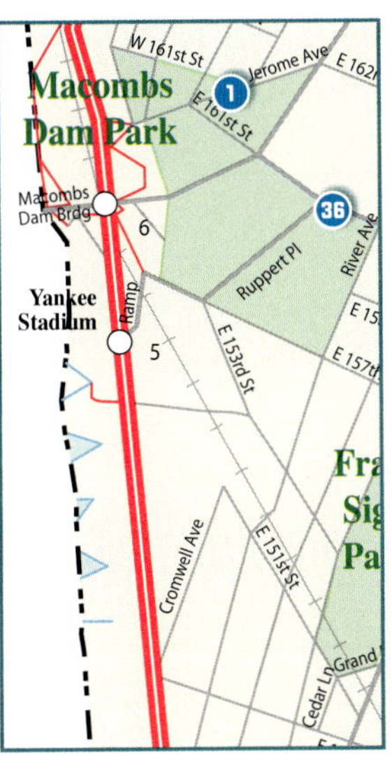
W 161st St
Jerome Ave
Macombs Dam Park
E 161st St
Macombs Dam Brdg
6
Ruppert Pl
River Ave
Yankee Stadium
Ramp
5
E 153rd St
Cromwell Ave
E 151st St
Cedar Ln
Grand

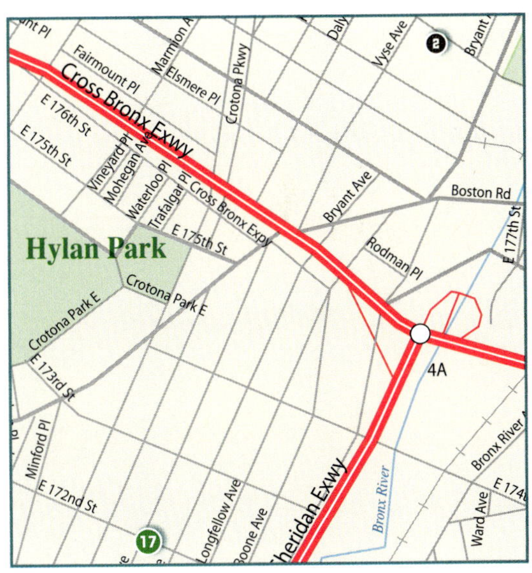
Fairmount Pl
Marmion Ave
Elsmere Pl
Crotona Pkwy
Daly
Vyse Ave
Bryant
Cross Bronx Exwy
E 176th St
E 175th St
Vineyard Pl
Mohegan Ave
Waterloo Pl
Trafalgar Pl
Cross Bronx Expy
Bryant Ave
Boston Rd
Hylan Park
E 175th St
Rodman Pl
E 177th St
Crotona Park E
Crotona Park E
4A
E 173rd St
Minford Pl
Bronx River
E 172nd St
Longfellow Ave
Boone Ave
Sheridan Exwy
Ward Ave

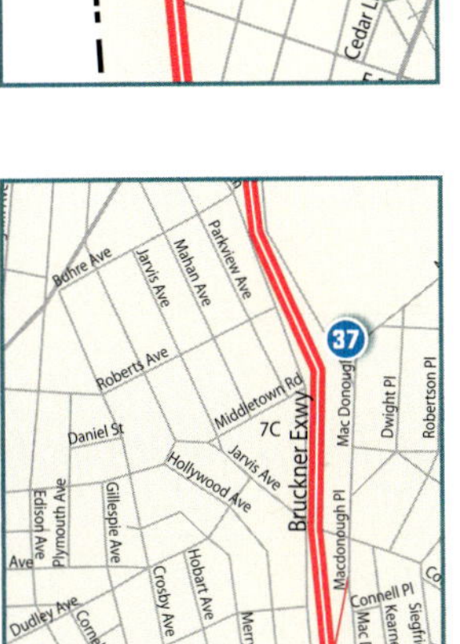
Bohre Ave
Jarvis Ave
Mahan Ave
Parkview Ave
Roberts Ave
Middletown Rd
7C
Mac Donough
Dwight Pl
Robertson Pl
Daniel St
Jarvis Ave
Hollywood Ave
Bruckner Exwy
Macdonough Pl
Edison Ave
Plymouth Ave
Gillespie Ave
Crosby Ave
Hobart Ave
Dudley Ave
Cornell Pl
Merry Av
Connell Pl
Mac Don
Kearney A
Siegfried P

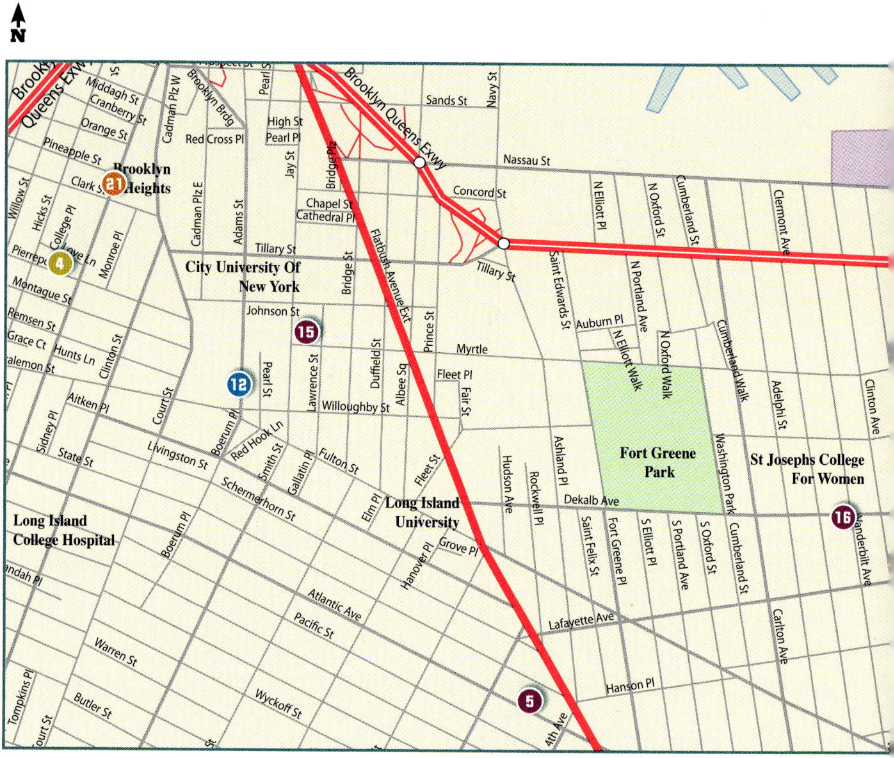

N
Brooklyn Queens Exwy
Middagh St
Cranberry St
Orange St
Pineapple St
Clark St
Brooklyn Heights
21
Willow St
Hicks St
College Pl
Love Ln
Pierrepont
4
Monroe Pl
Montague St
Remsen St
Grace Ct
Hunts Ln
Joralemon St
Clinton St
Cadman Plz W
Brooklyn Brdg
Red Cross Pl
Pearl St
High St
Pearl Pl
Jay St
Cadman Plz E
Adams St
Bridge Plz
Chapel St
Cathedral Pl
Tillary St
City University Of New York
Johnson St
15
12
Pearl St
Lawrence St
Bridge St
Flatbush Avenue Ext
Duffield St
Albee Sq
Willoughby St
Prince St
Myrtle
Fleet Pl
Fair St
Sands St
Navy St
Nassau St
Concord St
Tillary St
N Elliott Pl
N Oxford St
Cumberland St
Clermont Ave
Saint Edwards St
Auburn Pl
N Portland Ave
N Elliott Walk
N Oxford Walk
Cumberland Walk
Adelphi St
Clinton Ave
Fort Greene Park
Washington Park
St Josephs College For Women
16
Vanderbilt Ave
Aitken Pl
Court St
Sidney Pl
State St
Livingston St
Boerum Pl
Red Hook Ln
Smith St
Gallatin Pl
Fulton St
Schermerhorn St
Elm Pl
Fleet St
Long Island University
Hudson Ave
Rockwell Pl
Ashland Pl
Dekalb Ave
Saint Felix St
Fort Greene Pl
S Elliott Pl
S Portland Ave
S Oxford St
Cumberland St
Long Island College Hospital
Boerum Pl
Hanover Pl
Grove Pl
Atlantic Ave
Pacific St
Lafayette Ave
Carlton Ave
Warren St
Hanson Pl
Tompkins Pl
Butler St
Wyckoff St
5
4th Ave

President St
22
Garfield Pl
Polhemus Pl
Fiske Pl
Lincoln Pl
Grand Army Plz
2nd St
Montgomery Pl
6th Ave
4th St
5th St
7th Ave
8th Ave
Prospect Park
Flatbush Ave
7th St
8th St
New York Methodist Hospital
14
3
1
Park

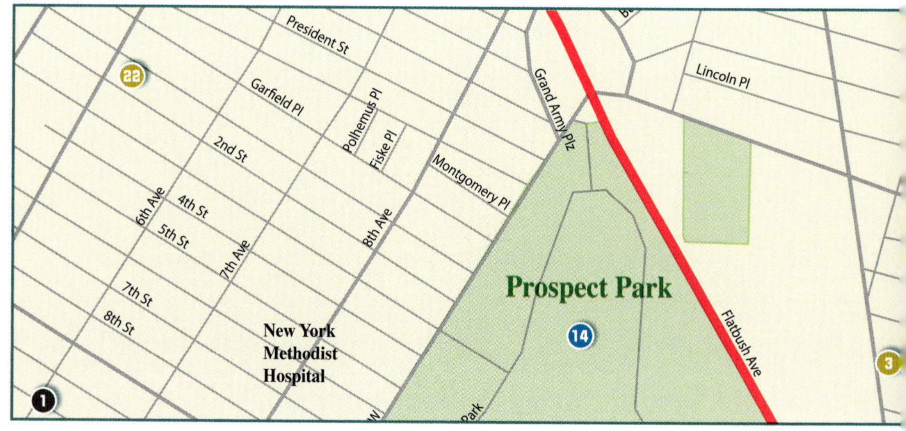

E 25th St
E 26th St
Clarendon Rd
oklyn Ave
New York
Nostrand Ave
Avenue D
Newkirk Ave
Victor Rd
s Ct
Foster Ave
11
Farragut Pl
Brooklyn Rd

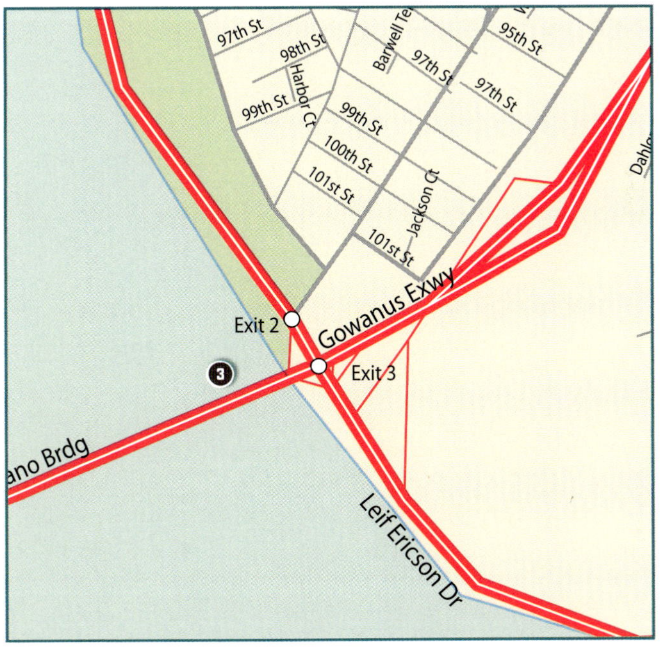

97th St
98th St
Barwell Te
95th St
Harbor Ct
97th St
97th St
99th St
99th St
100th St
101st St
Jackson Ct
101st St
Dahl
Gowanus Exwy
Exit 2
Exit 3
3
ano Brdg
Leif Ericson Dr

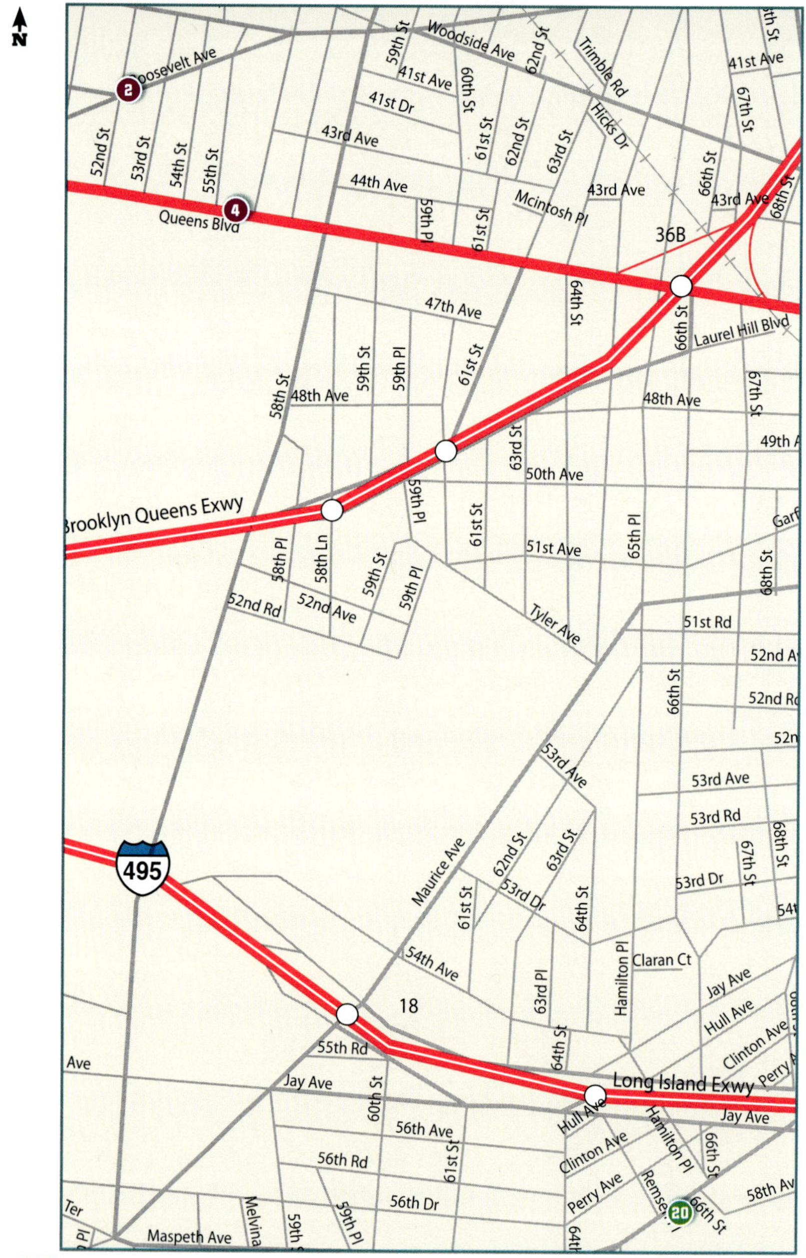

Roosevelt Ave
2
Woodside Ave
59th St
62nd St
Trimble Rd
41st Ave
41st Ave
60th St
67th St
41st Dr
Hicks Dr
52nd St
53rd St
54th St
55th St
43rd Ave
61st St
62nd St
63rd St
66th St
44th Ave
43rd Ave
Mcintosh Pl
43rd Ave
68th St
4
Queens Blvd
59th Pl
61st St
36B
64th St
47th Ave
66th St
Laurel Hill Blvd
58th St
59th St
59th Pl
61st St
48th Ave
48th Ave
67th St
63rd St
49th A
50th Ave
59th Pl
Brooklyn Queens Exwy
61st St
65th Pl
Garf
51st Ave
58th Pl
58th Ln
59th St
59th Pl
68th St
52nd Rd
52nd Ave
Tyler Ave
51st Rd
52nd A
66th St
52nd Rd
52n
53rd Ave
53rd Ave
53rd Rd
495
Maurice Ave
62nd St
63rd St
68th St
67th St
53rd Dr
53rd Dr
61st St
64th St
54t
54th Ave
Hamilton Pl
Claran Ct
63rd Pl
Jay Ave
Hull Ave
18
64th St
Clinton Ave
55th Rd
Ave
Perry A
Long Island Exwy
Jay Ave
60th St
Hull Ave
Jay Ave
Hamilton Pl
56th Ave
61st St
Clinton Ave
66th St
56th Rd
Perry Ave
Remsen Pl
58th Av
Ter
56th Dr
Melvina
59th Pl
59th St
20
66th St
Pl
Maspeth Ave
64th

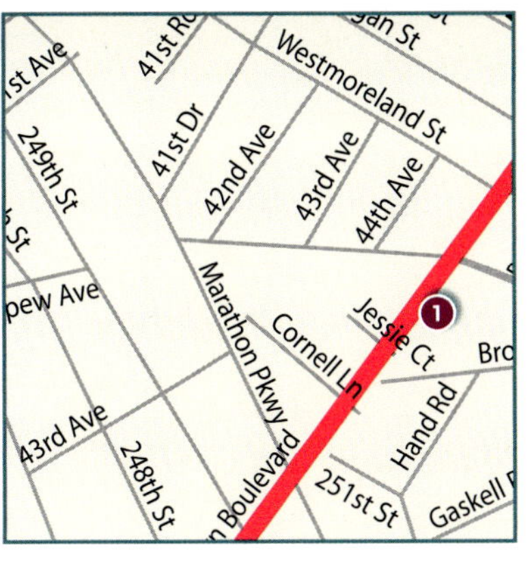

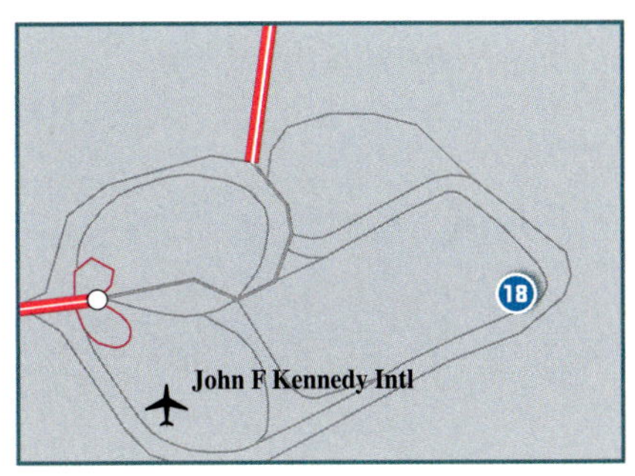

62nd Dr
65th Dr
66th Rd
66th Dr
70th St
71st St
72nd St
74th St
75th St
73rd Pl
65th Dr
Juniper Valley Rd
Gray St
77th St
66th Rd
66th Dr
78th St
79th St
80th St
St. John's Cemetery
4
Metropolitan Ave
67th Rd
67th Dr
68th Ave
68th Rd
69th Ave
69th Rd
69th Dr
76th St
68th Rd
69th Ave
Cook Ave
70th Ave
74th St
71st Ave
Cooper Ave
Valentine Pl
79th Pl
71st Ave
Aubrey Ave
Doran Ave
83rd St
84th St
73rd Ave
89th St
88th St
75th Ave
76th Ave
77th Ave
P A Railroad
Edsall Ave
Otto Rd
77th Ave
77th Rd
81st St
82nd St
83rd St
84th St
85th St
78th Ave
86th St
87th St
78th Rd
79th Pl
79th Ln
66th Pl
67th St
67th Pl
68th St
70th Ave
68th Pl
69th St
69th Pl
70th St
71st St
71st Pl
72nd St
72nd Pl
73rd St
Cooper Ave
73rd Pl
75th St
76th St
78th St
79th St
66th St
Central Ave
Access Rd
Interborough Pkwy
Myrtle Ave
Indiana Ave
72nd Ln
65th Pl
66th St
66th Pl
67th St
67th Pl
68th St
Cooper Ave
Luther Rd
Indiana Ave
65th St
80th Ave
Cypress Hills St
14
85th Rd
80th St
85th Ave
85th Rd
85th Dr

A Publication of the Foreign Excellent Trenchcoat Society, Inc.

Spy Sites of New York City is produced by becker&mayer!, Bellevue, Washington.
www.beckermayer.com

Designers: Matt Fisher and Megan Sugiyama
Editor: Betsy Henry Pringle
Production coordinator: Jennifer Marx
Managing editor: Amelia Riedler
12165
Printed in the United States of America

ISBN: 978-1-60380-261-1

All images and photographs are property and courtesy of the authors, except as noted below:

New York City maps © Creative Force Maps. Front cover: Ferenz/Shutterstock. Title page: SeanPavonePhoto/Shutterstock. Page 11: Franklin Join or Die image courtesy Library of Congress. Page 13: Nathan Hale statue courtesy of the New York City Parks Department. Page 18: Rivington *Royal Gazette* courtesy of New York Historical Society. Page 19: Robert Townsend image courtesy of the Collection of the Friends of Raynham Hall. Page 20: Fraunces Tavern photograph courtesy of Library of Congress. Page 23: Hamilton Grange photograph courtesy of the National Parks Service. Page 29: Tad Denson/Shutterstock. Page 39: Bambert Patrick/Shutterstock. Page 46: Sixty-Ninth Regiment Armory photograph courtesy of James P. Tierney, Colonel, U.S. Army (Retired), Regimental Historian, Sixty-Ninth Regiment, New York. Page 53: Wilson photograph courtesy of Library of Congress. Page 55: velora/Shutterstock, samodelkin8/Shutterstock. Page 60: Pierrepont Hotel photograph courtesy of Brooklyn Public Library, Brooklyn Collection. Page 83: Len Green/Shutterstock. Page 90: St. Regis Hotel photograph courtesy of The St. Regis New York. Page 95: Moe Berg photograph courtesy of National Baseball Hall of Fame Library. Page 97: The '21' Club photograph courtesy of The '21' Club. Page 99: The Dakota photograph courtesy of Library of Congress. Page 103: Oledjio/Shutterstock. Page 104: E. Michael Burke photograph courtesy of National Baseball Hall of Fame Library. Page 118: Grant's Tomb courtesy of National Parks Service. Page 122: David Marcus Theatre photograph courtesy of the Theatre Historical Society of America. Page 127: patrimonio designs limited/Shutterstock. Page 135: Chapman and Lazaro photographs courtesy of FBI. Paper textures used on front and back covers: R-studio/Shutterstock, AKaiser/Shutterstock. **Photographs by Henry R. Schlesinger:** Page 15: Battle of Harlem Heights plaque. Page 17: Mulligan gravestone. Page 21: Peck Slip. Page 24: Hamilton gravesite. Page 31: Bowser memorial. Page 45: New York Yacht club. Page 48: The Peninsula. Page 51: Trotsky residence. Page 52: Trotsky workplace. Page 56: SWP building. Page 57: Harte residence. Page 59: Arenal residence. Page 62: Daily Worker building. Page 64: Taft Hotel. Page 68: Dodd Stern residence. Page 70: Krivitsky residence. Page 74: Whitehall Building. Page 75: Knickerbocker Hotel. Page 77: Duquesne residence. Page 78: Vichy French offices. Page 82: Astor home. Page 86: Popov residence. Page 88: Affinia Manhattan Hotel. Page 89: Radisson Martinique Hotel. Page 92: Dickinson doll shop. Page 93: Dietrich residence. Page 94: McWilliams residence. Page 96: Plaza Hotel. Page 102: Dahl residence. Page 104: Grand Hyatt Hotel. Page 105: Riverdale compound. Page 106: Rosenberg residence. Page 107: Arkino Pictures. Page 109: Abel residence. Page 110: Latham Hotel. Page 111: Amtorg Trading Company. Page 113: Manhattan office building. Page 114: The Pennsylvania Hotel, 81 Bedford Street. Page 118: Straight residence. Page 119: Koecher residence. Page 120: United Nations building. Page 124: Grand Central Station; Church of the Transfiguration. Page 125: Israeli consulate. Page 129: Al-Farooq Mosque. Page 130: World Trade Center. Page 132: Parlor Maid residence. Page 133: Payoneer offices. Page 134: Columbus Circle. Page 136: Chapman residence. Page 137: NYPD 1st Precinct building. Page 139: Javits Federal Building. **Photographs by William Schlesinger:** Page 40: Black Chamber. Page 72: Theremin workshop. Page 84: BSC headquarters. Page 116: Ames residence. Page 131: Cuban Mission plaque. Back cover: Photograph of Henry R. Schlesinger.